Marriage Is for Keeps

Wedding Edition
with
Marriage Rite and Readings

John F. Kippley

The Foundation for the Family, Inc.
Cincinnati, Ohio

Publisher
Foundation for the Family, Inc.

Mailing address
P.O. Box 111184
Cincinnati OH 45211
513-471-2000
ccli@ccli.org

Nihil obstat
Rev. Edward J. Gratsch
3 September 1993

Imprimatur
Most Rev. Carl K. Moeddel
Auxiliary Bishop of the Archdiocese of Cincinnati
22 September 1993

> The *Nihil obstat* and the *Imprimatur* are a declaration that
> a book or pamphlet is considered to be free from doctrinal
> or moral error. It is not implied that those who have granted
> the *Nihil obstat* and *Imprimatur* agree with the contents,
> opinions or statements expressed.

Cataloging data
Dewey: 284.4
Library of Congress: 94-72395
ISBN: 0-926412-12-4

Kippley, John F.
Marriage Is for Keeps, Wedding Edition
1. Marriage   3. Sacraments
2. Christian marriage   4. Marriage counseling

Printing: 10   9

Table of Contents

Part II: The Rite of Marriage and Readings

Acknowledgements

Quotations from Sacred Scripture are from the Revised Standard Version Bible, Catholic Edition, © 1965 and 1966 by the Division of Christian Education of the National Council of the Churches of Christ in the U.S.A. Used by permission.

The Rite of Marriage is published by authority of the Committee on the Liturgy, National Conference of Catholic Bishops.

In Part II, the code numbers for the readings (i.e., A-1, B-1, etc.) correspond to The Rite of Marriage Ritual Cards published by Ave Maria Press, Notre Dame, Indiana 46556. When appropriate, the numbers in parentheses refer to the Lectionary numbers.

The English translation of the General Introduction, some Pslam responses, some Alleluia and Gospel verses, and the Lenten Gospel Acclamations, some Summaries, and the Titles and Conclusions of the Readings, from the *Lectionary for Mass* © 1968, 1981, 1997, International Committee on English in the Liturgy, Inc., Washington, D.C. All rights reserved.

Foreword

To the engaged couple:

If you are recently engaged and preparing to begin your life together, this is an exciting, wonderful, and special time in your life. Deep in your heart you realize that what is happening in your life is not an accident, it is not simply good luck, it is not fate. It is the Lord working in your life. One of the reasons God made you was so that you would become a Christian husband or wife and help your spouse on the path to the Kingdom of God. In a word, authentic Christian marriage is holy. And you are being called by the Lord to a new level of holiness.

When we look around our world today, we can also see that marriage, or what sociologists call "the institution of marriage," is in crisis. A couple entering into marriage in the United States in the 1990s, including nominally Catholic couples, has only about a 50 percent statistical "chance" of a successful, lasting marriage. You probably know friends or family who married for happiness but found misery instead. Why is it that some newlyweds barely survive life together past the honeymoon, while other newlyweds go on to celebrate their marriage for a lifetime? How is it that some people find themselves feeling so terribly hurt and disillusioned because of marriage, while others, even though they face all the burdens and troubles that are part of life, find themselves more in love after fifty years of marriage than they were on their wedding day? This little book will help you find the answers.

Before marrying in the Church, a couple must begin to ask and begin to answer some important questions: What are my values and priorities? What does commitment mean? What is the purpose of my life? What does it mean to be a husband, a wife, a man, a woman? Questions like these raise essentially spiritual issues. If you can begin to answer these questions in a mature, honest, and Christian way, you will find yourself on the road to a successful, happy, and life-giving marriage. Again, this little book will help you find the answers.

The first chapter of this book is the most difficult. But take the time to read it carefully. It is difficult because it will ask you to look honestly at yourself, to look toward the Lord, and to grow in your relationship with the Lord. There is a word for this — Discipleship. Several chapters offer you some good, common sense advice on things like finances, communication, and even your wedding plans. Pay close attention to the chapters dealing with sexuality, birth control, and natural family planning. Sexuality and spirituality are intimately connected. If you and your spouse strive to live your sexuality in a healthy, Christian manner, you will find that your marriage is not only successful; your marriage will also grow in love and holiness.

To priests, deacons, and marriage ministers:

You will find that this little book fills an important need in our parish marriage preparation or pre-Cana programs. It is a book that not only engaged couples but also clergy and lay ministers ought to read.

In helping engaged couples prepare for Christian marriage, there are three things we need to do. First is the ever present paperwork and requirements of civil and Church law. This is important, but it is not a central part of the chapters that follow. Second, there is the need to raise questions, lots and lots of questions. There are certain things that simply ought to be talked about before a couple enters marriage. The engaged couple does not necessarily have to prove anything to you. In fact the hours they spend alone talking to each other, after they have met the priest or marriage minister, are often more important than the time they spend talking with you. The word for all this is communication. There are already a number of good guides, personality profiles, and even computer printouts available to help couples learn communication skills. But this little book will help couples communicate about essential issues of marriage itself, issues like discipleship, birth control, and commitment.

The third thing we need to do is to teach. This is where this little book can fill a great need in your parish pre-Cana program. Our Catholic Church has a wealth of experience and wisdom in the areas of sexuality, fertility, marriage and family. Often our Church marriage preparation programs are quite good at helping engaged couples learn communication skills, but just as often we do not adequately communicate the Catholic experience, teaching and wisdom concerning marriage. In a clear, easy to understand manner the chapters that follow will talk to the reader about authentic Christian marriage.

Every engaged couple can benefit by reading this little book. In fact it would make excellent reading for seminary or college classes on marriage and family life. Give this book to the engaged couples in your parish and talk to them about what it says. Suggest that they keep it in their homes to read again as problems or issues arise and again as they grow in Christian marriage.

Fr. Gerard P. Hiland

Introduction

Why was this book written?

Various priests suggested that it would be helpful to have a small book that gave sufficient attention to the three most important aspects of preparing for marriage: discipleship, indissolubility, and marital chastity. They also wanted it to cover those matters that have become traditional in contemporary preparation for marriage — communication, finances, the wedding ceremony, etc.

Aren't all of these subjects well covered in pre-Cana programs?

It has been my personal experience that teaching about indissolubility and marital chastity sometimes has fallen through the cracks despite plenty of good will. For example, parish priests may think that these subjects are being adequately taught at the diocesan sponsored pre-Cana program or similar sessions, and the people who run those programs may think that these important matters are being covered by the parish priests. In some cases, both assumptions may be wrong. In other cases, the contents of this book will simply provide a written supplement to what you are learning in your face to face sessions.

Why should we as an engaged couple take the time to read and discuss this book?

As you reflect upon the effort you put into getting whatever education you have, you most likely will agree that the success you had in any difficult course was proportional to the amount of preparation you put into it. If you engaged in competitive athletics, you know that success is impossible without adequate preparation.

You are now planning to marry. You know that last year and five and ten years ago, millions of other couples married and that some of them are now very unhappy; some are even divorced. No one wants you to become a statistic of marital unhappiness and divorce. Both you and your priest or deacon want you to enter the ranks of those who learn to strengthen their love within marriage and who remain happily married in the face of the inevitable difficulties that married couples encounter.

So why not prepare well for marriage? If you spent some hours, or even many hours, just to get through one high school or college course, be prepared to spend some time preparing for the commitment that lasts for a lifetime and which entails a whole new way of life.

Look at it this way. Don't you need to discuss what's involved in Christian marriage—before you marry? This little book provides a format, a way to start. It can help you begin to discuss the really important aspects of Christian marriage—discipleship, the absolute permanence of true marriage, and purity of mind, heart and body within marriage. The discussion questions at the end of the chapters were drafted by a reviewer who has had years of experience in helping couples get ready for marriage. They're starters; please use them.

How should we use this book?

Since it's short, you could read it all in one or two evenings, but I suggest a slower approach. Perhaps your priest or deacon will ask you to read and discuss three or four chapters between each of your scheduled meetings with him. Or perhaps you and your fiance will read and discuss one chapter each week. Develop a plan and keep to it.

Is it easy reading?

Well, how are we doing so far? Some of the first chapters are a bit heavy. Sorry about that, but what can be more serious and important than your permanent relationships with God and with each other? With a mostly question-answer format, I tried to make this readable.

Is this book for couples where one person isn't Catholic?

Very definitely yes. If you are preparing for a religiously mixed marriage, I hope you will **both** read and discuss this book. Marriage is first a natural institution before being raised to the supernatural level in Christian matrimony, and I think there's much here for the person who does not share the full Catholic faith. Also, both parties should understand the Catholic spouse's obligation to follow the teaching of the Catholic Church.

You may find certain chapters more meaningful after a few months or years of married life, so please keep this book for future reference.

I hope and I pray that in your marriage you will grow in Christian holiness and that we may have the pleasure of meeting in heaven.

John F. Kippley

1. Marriage and Discipleship

First things first

You're planning to enter a Christian marriage. Rather obviously, that's a marriage which has something to do with Jesus Christ. It's a marriage in which at least one of the spouses is Christian.

So, what's a Christian? In one sense, every validly baptized person is a Christian, and that's an important meaning of the word. However, in everyday talk, you hear people talk about *real* Christians as contrasted with *nominal* Christians.

By real Christians they mean those who take seriously what it means to be a Christian. In other words—discipleship—what it means to be a disciple of the Lord Jesus. By nominal Christians they mean people who wear the label but don't let it affect their day-to-day lives. Using such labels may sound uncharitable at first, but it's actually very much in line with what Jesus taught:

> Not everyone who says to me, "Lord, Lord," shall enter the
> kingdom of heaven, but he who does the will of my Father
> who is in Heaven (Mt 7:21).

If you're going to enter Christian marriage, then doesn't it make sense to take a few moments to review what's involved in being Christian? That's putting first things first.

". . . And the truth shall make you free."

How many times have you heard that statement without any reference as to who said it? Do you know who said it? Do you know the rest of the sentence that preceded the words ". . . and the truth shall make you free"? Let's take a look.

> Jesus then said to the Jews who had believed in Him, "If
> you continue in my word, you are truly my disciples, and
> you will know the truth, and the truth will make you free"
> (John 8:32).

What that means is this: to be truly free, you have to know the truth; in order to know the truth, you have to be a disciple of Jesus; and to be a disciple, you have to continue in his word.

1

To be a disciple. . .

What does it mean to be a disciple? The word disciple comes from the Latin word meaning "to learn." To be a disciple means that you realize you need to learn from a teacher. To be a **Christian** disciple means you are ready and willing to learn from Jesus. It means that with your heart and your mind you realize you are a sinner and that you cannot save yourself. True Christian discipleship means that you accept Jesus as your Lord and personal savior and that you believe in Jesus with your whole heart and soul; it means that you accept Him for what He claims to be: "I am the way, and the truth, and the life; no one comes to the Father but by Me" (Jn 14:6).

A change of heart

There's another side to the coin, too. A university fundraising videotape opened with a young woman saying,

> I just love it here. The first day of class, our philosophy instructor told us, "From now on you are going to think for yourselves. No one is going to tell you what's right and wrong."

Really? What about Jesus? Can a Christian say to *Him*: You're not going to tell me what's right or wrong?"

If you apply to Christ the attitude expressed in that videotape scene, you are not a disciple of Jesus. The attitude of the Christian disciple has to be, "Lord, teach me what is right and wrong, and please give me the grace to accept your teaching and to follow You."

As a Christian, you have been blessed with the grace of faith and have been given a special relationship with Jesus at baptism, but it is possible that you have not given much thought about what it means to be a disciple of Jesus. I find a handy reminder of who Jesus is in this little poem which I generally receive on a Christmas card each year.

One Solitary Life

He was born in an obscure village,
the child of a peasant woman.
He worked in a carpenter shop
and was an itinerant preacher.
He never wrote a book.
He never held an office.

He did none of the things
one usually associates with greatness.
Nineteen centuries have come and gone,
and today He is the central figure
of the human race.
All the armies that ever marched,
all the navies that ever sailed,
all the kings that ever reigned,
put together,
have not affected
the life of man on this earth
as much as that
ONE SOLITARY LIFE.

Pride and self-sufficiency

Jesus knew that the biggest obstacle to following Him would be an attitude of pride and self-sufficiency. It has always been that way. Look at how Satan tempted our parents, Adam and Eve: "You will be like God, knowing good and evil" (Gen 3:5). In other words, you won't have to listen to God; you will know for yourself what is right and wrong. It was the Big Lie from the father of lies then, and it's still the Big Lie today. Eve and then Adam refused God their willingness to look to Him for the truth and to obey Him, and we call that the Original Sin. But in our own way, we repeat it every time we refuse to look to God for the truth about right and wrong and refuse to obey Him.

Our first parents, acting on our behalf, lost the life of grace for themselves and for us. Jesus came to save us from the effects of their sin and our own. St. John the Evangelist put it succinctly:

For God so loved the world that he gave his only Son, that whoever believes in Him should not perish but have eternal life (Jn 3:16).

Jesus, knowing full well the problem of pride and self-sufficiency, attacked it from the beginning of his public life. Mark tells us that He began his preaching with this basic message: "The kingdom of God is at hand; repent, and believe in the gospel" (Mk 1:15). "Repent" is better translated as "Have a change of heart." Repentance has to do with our past sins, and there is no question that being sorry for our past sins is a very important part of an overall change of heart. However, Jesus is forward looking; He is more

3

interested in our present and our future than our past, and the phrase "have a change of heart" gives us a better idea of what we have to do to become his disciples.

If you are prepared to have that change of heart—and it's something we have to keep working at all our lives, then you understand what Jesus was talking about when He taught: "Unless you turn [have a change of heart] and become like children, you will never enter the kingdom of heaven. Whoever humbles himself like this child, he is the greatest in the kingdom of heaven" (Mt 18:3-4). What is the characteristic we love best in little children? Surely it has to be their openness, their realistic dependence on their parents, their willingness to learn from their parents and teachers, their lack of pretense at being great, and it's clear from the context that this is what Jesus was teaching about.

The glory and the price of discipleship

We love to hear St. Paul quote the prophet Isaiah, "Eye has not seen nor has it entered into the mind of man what God has prepared for those who love him" (1Cor 2:9).

If we have much experience with life, we take great comfort in the call of Jesus: "Come to Me, all who labor and are heavy laden, and I will give you rest. Take my yoke upon you and learn from Me; for I am gentle and lowly in heart, and you will find rest for your souls. For my yoke is easy and my burden is light" (Mt 11:28-30).

At the same time, we know that the universal symbol of being Christian is the cross. "If any man would come after Me, let him deny himself and take up his cross daily and follow Me" (Lk 9:23).

Then there follows in the same passage—the very next verse—one of the great practical truths taught by Jesus: "For whoever would save his life will lose it; and whoever loses his life for my sake, he will save it." Who could say that except the God-man? If I said it or if you said it, people would rightly think we were crazy. It is one of the indirect ways in which Jesus taught about who He was and is—true God as well as true man. What it means is both simple and profound: if we refuse the cross of discipleship in the pursuit of money and pleasure—even the pleasures of marriage, we will lose eternal life; on the other hand, if we are willing to die to self and to walk with Jesus in this life, we will be with Him for all eternity.

Jesus concludes this teaching with a statement that has truly been life-changing for many: "What will it profit a man if he gains the whole world and forfeits his life?" (Mt 16:26) As you prepare for marriage, what greater realities might you consider?

He taught in a similar way in the Sermon on the Mount: "Enter by the narrow gate, for the gate is wide and the way is easy that leads to destruction, and those who enter by it are many. For the gate is narrow and the way is hard that leads to life, and those who find it are few" (Mt 7:13-14). Scholars tell us that "few" really means "not all," but the teaching still remains sobering. It is definitely possible for you and for me to refuse the way of the narrow gate and to walk the easy road that leads to destruction.

Can you admit your sinfulness?

A prime requirement for being an adult Christian is the willingness to admit, "I have sinned." Even the great saints acknowledged their sinfulness, even if in their cases it was more a recognition of their imperfections and the great distance between themselves and the absolute holiness of God. However, for most of us, it's a matter of admitting that in certain thoughts and desires, words, and actions, we have sinned against God and frequently against our fellow man. Simon Peter, when he first recognized that Jesus was truly a Man of God after witnessing the miracle of the catch of fish, said to Jesus: "Depart from me, for I am a sinful man, O Lord" (Lk 5:8).

It's relatively easy to admit our sinfulness in very general terms, but for *real* repentance, sorrow, and a change of heart, it's necessary for us to accuse ourselves of the *specific* sins we have committed.

This is hard for anyone because it takes humility. It's pretty easy for someone to admit that he or she has been missing Sunday Mass because that's so obvious to family and friends. It's something else to accuse oneself of *sin* against the Third Commandment by such behavior. An employee might openly joke about stealing from his employer by taking "sick days" for just a day off, but it's hard to accuse oneself of sin by such behavior. Why? I think most of us recognize that when we admit we are sinning, we should undergo that change of heart and behavior to which Jesus is calling us.

Self-accusation can be particularly hard for some engaged persons because they may be committing various sins of impurity—fornication (that's the biblical name for unmarried people having sex), masturbation, deliberately getting oneself or the other aroused, and leading another person into sin. Sins of sex can form very strong and bad habits. It is difficult enough for anyone to be chaste in thought, word and deed; the force of bad habit makes it even more difficult. It is easy to become a slave to one's own sinful habits of sex, and that's all the more reason to turn to Jesus, to answer his call to have a change of heart—now, not later.

5

If you and your intended spouse are engaging in immoral behavior, isn't it time to admit to yourselves that such behavior is completely contradictory to the way of Jesus, and isn't it time to have that necessary change of heart and behavior?

How can you do it?

If you know the demands of the Christian moral life and are also aware of your own weakness and sins, you may ask, "Well, how can I, weak as I am, walk the narrow way with Jesus?" The answer is simple: by yourself you can't do it, but with the help of Jesus you can. St. Paul tells us that he was very unhappy about a certain trial which he called "a messenger of Satan, to harass me, to keep me from being too elated. Three times I besought the Lord about this, that it should leave me; but He said to me, 'My grace is sufficient for you, for my power is made perfect in weakness' " (2Cor 12:7-9).

What was true for St. Paul is equally true for me and for you.

The assurance of forgiveness

For many of us sinners, two of the most encouraging parables of Jesus are those of the Good Shepherd and the Prodigal Son. In the first, Jesus tells us of God's pursuit of the sinner and of the joy in heaven over the repentant sinner (Mt 18:12-14). The parable of the Prodigal Son (Lk 15:11-32) is longer and more complete. The young man leaves home to lead an immoral life. Finally he comes to his senses. Then comes a crucial point: he accuses himself of his sins:

> I will arise and go to my father, and I will say to him,
> "Father, I have sinned against heaven and before you; I am
> no longer worthy to be called your son; treat me as one of
> your hired servants."

Then he makes his confession to his father who rejoices to forgive him.

The Sacrament of Reconciliation

Because we are sinners, Jesus gave us the Sacrament of Reconciliation to do just what the name says — to reconcile us with God through the good agency of his Church. One of the best resolutions you can make as an engaged couple is to go to confession once a month starting now and for the rest of your life. You don't need to be concerned about telling the priest something he hasn't heard before. Many people find sins of impurity particularly difficult to confess. Well, yes, they are embarrassing and they're such a reminder of our weakness; but, no, they won't surprise the priest. A priest-reviewer of this book added the rest of this paragraph as follows: Even the youngest priest has been trained to expect weakness and falls in such matters and not to judge harshly persons who have been overtaken by sexual impulses in an unguarded moment or out of compulsive habits. Moreover, even if the priest himself has by a special protection of God never fallen into a serious sexual sin (and not all priests have been so fortunate), he is aware enough of his own weakness not to feel morally superior to a brother or sister who has had a fall.

Repentance plus healing

It is tremendously important for each of us to realize that God's Commandments are for our benefit, not his. They spell out some very basic relationships between you and God, and between you and other people. To violate the Commandments is to act against your very nature as someone created in the image and likeness of God.

Have you ever heard it said, "What you don't know won't hurt you"? Try telling that to someone who's been poisoned by eating the wrong kind of mushrooms! What a lie! The truth is, what you don't know can hurt you very much indeed.

For example, maybe it's out of ignorance that some couples have sex before they marry. Maybe they don't know it's objectively sinful behavior. (Maybe. But why do they try to "justify" it? Nobody has to justify honest *marital* relations.) Regardless, having sex outside of marriage does cause spiritual damage to both persons, and that damage needs healing. Sometimes the psychological damage can be so severe that it affects a person's ability to make the necessary consent to lifelong, faithful marriage. It is no surprise that couples who cohabit before marriage have a higher divorce rate than those who don't.

The point of all this is that if you have been engaging in premarital sex, you need healing. For your own sakes, you need to repent, to be reconciled with God, and to be healed. You need to develop a chaste courtship, perhaps even some separation and some special time with God to facilitate your healing.

If this applies to you and yours, you will find the confessional is a good place to find peace and a fresh start.

Walking with the Lord — together

Living out the Sacrament of Matrimony is a special form of Christian discipleship. It is very definitely a vocation, a calling from the Lord, but it is not a calling just to "get married" and then forget about the active practice of the Faith except for a few big occasions such as Christmas and Easter, baptisms and weddings.

When you enter the Sacrament of Matrimony, you and your spouse are both called to walk with the Lord — together. For a mental image, envision yourself and your spouse walking with Jesus, He in the middle and each of you holding one of his hands. That is what successful, happy Christian marriage is all about.

In the Catholic vision of living together as man and wife, *you both agree that the essential purpose of your marriage is to help each other reach your goal of eternal life.* You both agree that it's important for you to be aware of the need to help each other on the road to heaven.

If such an idea of marriage is meaningless to you or to your intended spouse, then don't you need to ask yourself why you are entering **Christian** marriage? If you or your intended spouse have entirely different and even unreconcilable opinions about Christian discipleship or about letting Jesus be King and Center of your personal and married lives, then don't you need to ask yourselves if you are being called by the Lord to marry each other?

Some couples may prefer not to think about their proposed marriage in the light of Christian discipleship, and that might apply to you. But what if you and your proposed spouse have some very serious differences about the need to let Jesus have dominion over your lives together? What if you are telling yourself that since you have come this far without such differences creating a problem, you're sure that everything will be just fine until death do you part?

Any experienced marriage counselor, especially a Christian one, would say, "Don't kid yourselves. That's a very dangerous assumption."

If the above should apply to you, the first thing you need to do is to ask yourself if one reason Christian discipleship hasn't been a sore point between you and your fiance might be that, well, you haven't been much of a disciple. Could it be that aside from lip service and Sunday Mass, there hasn't been anything in your behavior—especially the things you do together—to distinguish you from an atheist?

I can assure you that the glow of the time of courtship will not keep you on a constant high for long. Sooner or later, religion—Christian discipleship—will become important either to you or to your spouse. If the fact that Christ died to save you and to bring you to eternal life is important to you, and if you plan to marry someone who is a practical atheist (even if he or she is a baptized Catholic), you can rest assured that your differences will become much more important to you in the years to come. Even if you happen to be a totally non-religious person, a practical atheist, planning to marry a non-practicing Catholic, the spark of faith in that person may not remain dormant forever. (A practical atheist is a person who believes that God exists but doesn't let that faith affect his or her personal, family, and social life in any significant way.)

Christian marriage is the vocation to walk together with the Lord, helping each other on the path of salvation, and raising children in the ways of the Lord. It is the way in which most Christians are called to live out their discipleship.

Discuss with your fiance:

1. Do we both agree that the long-range purpose of our marriage is to help each other reach our goal of eternal life?

2. What specific change of heart or change in behavior is necessary for us to walk more fully in the way of the Lord?

3. What habits do we need to develop or change — now — in order to live our marriage in Christian discipleship?

4. How do we plan to give practical recognition to our belief that marriage is a three-way relationship of man-woman-God?

2. Why Get Married in the Church?

The question in the title can have two different meanings. First, it can refer to having the wedding in the church building as contrasted with having it outdoors or at a hotel, and the answer can be brief: the basic reason for having your wedding in the church building is that the in-the-church wedding helps to emphasize the serious religious significance of marriage.

The second possible meaning of the title question has to do with being a Catholic. Why should Catholics have their marriage officially witnessed by a priest? The short and simple answer is that Catholics are bound to abide by the marriage laws of the Church. The longer answer really gets down to a fundamental question: why should you or I be Catholic and therefore be concerned about being married in the Church? That's what the rest of this chapter is about.

Why are you a Catholic?

Perhaps you were born into a Catholic family and were baptized into the Church very early in life, and you find it hard to say much more beyond that. While that's a starting point, you should be able to give a reason for an adult faith just as an adult convert does. The history of the Church is filled with the conversions of adults. Even today, some have given up very successful careers as Anglican or Protestant clergymen in order to enter the fullness of the Catholic Church. What leads such people to embrace the Catholic Faith?

The long answer is found in the books that many of them have written; the short answer is very simple and is what every convert and informed Catholic believes: Jesus Christ established the Catholic Church as his chosen way to keep alive his way, his truth, and his life.

Did Jesus really establish a visible, structured Church?

Most certainly, yes. The notion of an invisible and unstructured church is best described as a reactionary daydream, for it has no basis in the Bible or history. In the Old Testament, God took over 1,900 years from the call of Abraham to the birth of Jesus to build the Church of the Old Covenant, and it was certainly a visible and structured people of God.

The second person of the Blessed Trinity took on our visible human nature to complete the work of the Old Covenant and to establish the New Covenant in his own blood. In establishing the Church of the New Covenant, Jesus continued the same plan that He as God had already established in the

11

Church of the Old Covenant. He formed the Twelve Apostles as a special group. He taught with authority and He gave this authority to his apostles. "He who hears you, hears Me, and he who rejects you, rejects Me, and he who rejects Me rejects Him who sent Me" (Luke 10:16). He gave them special visible ways or means for the sanctification of his people. Right within the Twelve, He gave them the basic structure that endures unto this very day by giving Peter the special role of headship.

What was the role of Peter among the Twelve?

Jesus made Peter the head among the Twelve, and the headship of Peter was clearly recognized by the rest of the apostles and the whole early Church. The relationship between Peter and the Eleven after the Resurrection was and remains the relationship between the Pope, the Bishop of Rome, and the other bishops of the Church throughout the world. Peter and the others were all apostles, but Christ gave to Peter a distinctive role of headship. The Pope and the other bishops are all successors of the apostles, but the Pope is the successor of St. Peter and has that same role of Peter's headship that Christ Himself established.

What are the Biblical foundations for Peter's headship?

The gospels give us three foundational texts of Jesus, and the Acts of the Apostles has numerous accounts which illustrate the headship of Peter. In addition, every list of the Twelve Apostles starts with Peter. Let's take a look at the special things that Jesus said and did to Peter.

> Now when Jesus came into the district of Caesarea Philippi, He asked his disciples, "Who do men say that the Son of man is?" And they said, "Some say John the Baptist, others say Elijah, and others Jeremiah or one of the prophets." He said to them, "But who do you say that I am?"
>
> Simon Peter replied, "You are the Christ, the Son of the living God."
>
> And Jesus answered him, "Blessed are you, Simon Bar-Jona! For flesh and blood has not revealed this to you, but my Father who is in heaven. And I tell you, you are Peter, and on this rock I will build my Church and the gates of Hades shall not prevail against it. I will give you the keys of the kingdom of heaven, and whatever you bind on

earth shall be bound in heaven, and whatever you loose on
earth shall be loosed in heaven" (Mt 16:13-19).

Up until this time, there was no Jew with the name of Peter. Before this,
parents did not name their baby a rock. (Anti-Catholic skeptics at one time
tried to prove that Peter was a common name but proved just the opposite:
no Jew had been named Peter before this event.) The man who made the act
of faith in the messiahship and divinity of Christ was called Simon Bar-Jona
which means Simon, son of John. Jesus changed his name.

Peter is a translation of the Greek word for rock, petra. The change of
name designated a change of reality and is a direct parallel with what God
had done in forming the Church of the Old Covenant.

Remember that "Yahweh," as He named Himself to the Hebrews, called
a man named Abram (Gen 12:1), and eventually Yahweh changed his name
to Abraham which means the father of a multitude (Gen 17:5), for that was
what Yahweh had made him even though Abraham was 99 years old and his
son Isaac had not yet been conceived. And Yahweh kept his promise.

Jesus changed the name and therefore the reality of Simon to Rock, and
then He promised to build his Church upon that same Rock: "And on this
rock I will build My Church." And Jesus kept that promise, too.

Second, at the Last Supper Jesus gave Simon Peter the special role of
strengthening the rest of the Apostles. Note that this was not because of any
special virtue of Simon. Far from it. This mandate was given to Simon at
the same time that Jesus predicted Peter's betrayal. This is a powerful and
never-ending statement that the headship of Peter and his successors, the
popes, is not due to their personal virtue but is simply and solely due to the
will of Christ.

> Simon, Simon, behold, Satan demanded to have you [apostles]
> that he might sift you [all] like wheat, but I have prayed for
> you [personally] that your faith may not fail; and when you
> have turned again, strengthen your brethren.
>
> And he said to Him, "Lord, I am ready to go with you
> to prison and to death." He said, "I tell you, Peter, the cock
> will not crow this day until you three times deny that you
> know Me" (Lk 22:31-34). [Words in brackets reflect the Greek
> plural and singular of "you."]

The third foundation in the gospels is the account of the conversation
between Jesus and Simon Peter after the Resurrection (Jn 21:15-17). Three

13

times Jesus asks Simon Peter if he loves Him, and three times Peter replies, "Yes, Lord, you know that I love you." In response to the first affirmation of love, Jesus tells Peter, "Feed my lambs." To the second, "Tend my sheep." To the third, "Feed my sheep." Jesus had often spoken of Himself as the Good Shepherd and of his believers as his flock. Now He transmits to Simon Peter the responsibility for being the chief shepherd, and that remains the role of the Pope today.

The Acts of the Apostles contains too many illustrations of the headship of Peter to mention in this brief account, but a few can be listed. On Pentecost, it is Peter who is the spokesman (Acts 2:14-42). It is Peter who works the first miracle of healing and explains it (Acts 3). It is Peter who is called by the Lord to admit the first Gentiles into the Church (Acts 10). And when there was a dispute that needed to be settled, it is Peter who provides the authoritative answer (Acts 15:1-12).

Sacred Scripture makes it abundantly clear that the Church which Christ established was built on Peter—the Rock, and the headship of Peter continues in his successors, the Popes.

Why are the Pope and the central government of the Church in Rome?

Peter carried the message of Christ to Rome which was the center of civilization and government in his day; he was the apostle to Rome and was martyred there. (A church was built over his grave, and today that church has grown into St. Peter's Basilica.) The succeeding bishops of Rome have always been recognized as the successors to the headship of Peter, and this was true even at the very beginning when some of the other apostles were still living. For example, when the beloved Apostle John was still living, Pope Clement, the third successor of Peter, wrote to the Church of Corinth a letter to correct abuses which had been brought to his attention, and he clearly expected to be obeyed:

> If anyone disobey the things which have been said by Him
> [the Lord Jesus Christ] through us, let them know that they
> will involve themselves in transgression and in no small
> danger.[1]

Furthermore, it was recognized very early that if there was any confusion about what to teach and believe, you only needed to look to Rome. St. Irenaeus, Bishop of Lyons, writing about the year 190, stressed both the unity of Catholic faith and the primacy of the Church of Rome.

The Church . . . believes these things as if she had but one soul and one and the same heart, as if she possessed but one mouth. For while the languages of the world are diverse, nevertheless, the authority of the tradition is one and the same. Neither do the Churches among the Germans believe otherwise or have another tradition, nor do those among the Iberians, nor among the Celts, nor away in the East, nor in Egypt, nor in Libya, nor those which have been established in the central regions of the world.[2]

Addressing the question of how you can find the true apostolic teaching a century or so after the death of the last Apostle, Irenaeus wrote:

But since it would be too long to enumerate in such a volume as this the successions of all the Churches, we shall confound all those who, in whatever manner, whether through self-satisfaction or vainglory, or through blindness and wicked opinion, assemble other than where it is proper, by pointing out here the successions of the bishops of the greatest and most ancient Church known to all, founded and organized at Rome by the two most glorious Apostles, Peter and Paul, that Church which has the tradition and the faith which comes down to us after having been announced to men by the Apostles. For with this Church, because of its superior origin, all Churches must agree, that is, all the faithful in the whole world; and it is in her that the faithful everywhere have maintained the Apostolic tradition.[3]

How does Jesus continue to work through his Church?

In his own person, Jesus was and is Prophet, King, and Priest, and Jesus continues all these works in his Church. The traditional way of saying this is that Jesus, the Head, continues to teach, rule and sanctify in and through his Body, the Church.

To teach. The last thing Jesus did before He ascended into heaven was to reaffirm the tasks He had given to the Apostles and their successors:

All authority in heaven and on earth has been given to me.
Go therefore and make disciples of all nations, baptizing them in the name of the Father and of the Son and of the

15

Holy Spirit, teaching them to observe all that I have commanded you; and lo, I am with you always, to the close of the age (Mt 28:18-20).

Through his Church, Jesus continues to teach us what to believe and how to live, i.e., faith and morals.

To rule. Any organization on this earth from the individual family to the Catholic Church throughout the world needs legitimate authority and order, or there will be chaos. Within the Catholic Church, the supreme teaching and organizational authority resides with the Pope and the bishops in union with him, and this order was clearly established by Jesus.

If you hear someone say, "I don't like the Church always telling me what to do," you are listening to someone who is either very misinformed about the Church or simply does not want to listen to the Church doing its job of teaching the Commandments and leading us to do certain things together as a united family. This kind of leadership means making at least some rules. In point of fact, however, apart from teaching us to observe all that the Lord has commanded, the Church has very few other rules that affect the Catholic who is not a priest or nun. These rules are called the Six Precepts of the Church, and I list them here simply to illustrate that they are not extensive or burdensome.

1. To participate at Mass every Sunday and holy day of obligation.

2. To receive the Sacrament of Reconciliation at least once a year (if you have committed a mortal sin).

3. To receive the Sacrament of the Holy Eucharist at least once during the Easter time (the first Sunday of Lent through Trinity Sunday, the week after Pentecost).

4. To keep holy the holy days of obligation.

5. To fast and abstain from meat on the days appointed.

6. To contribute to the support of the Church.

The reason that most practicing Catholics cannot recite these six precepts is that they don't "feel" them as any sort of rule or commandment; they are simply the things that a practicing Catholic does as a matter of course.

To sanctify. Jesus has given us seven ordinary means for conferring upon us his life of sanctifying grace, and we call these the seven sacraments: Baptism, Reconciliation, Holy Eucharist, Confirmation, Matrimony, Holy

Orders, and the Anointing of the Sick. In addition, Jesus continues, through his Church and his word in Scripture, to urge us to daily prayer and to carry our daily cross including acts of voluntary self-denial.

What assurances has Jesus given us that what the Church teaches is true?

It's a matter of religious common sense that after teaching and even dying for the truth Jesus would not leave his followers without a firm and easy way to know the truth. That sure way is the specific teaching of the Church which He established.

Moreover, at the Last Supper, He repeatedly promised that He would not leave us orphans. Instead, He promised the Twelve Apostles that He would send the Holy Spirit upon them to lead them into the fullness of the truth. For example,

> These things I have spoken to you, while I am still with you. But the Counselor, the Holy Spirit, whom the Father will send in my name, He will teach you all things, and bring to your remembrance all that I have said to you (Jn 14:25-26).

Similar promises are recorded in John 14:16-17; 15:26-27; 16:12-13.

Catholic faith ultimately boils down to this: Catholics believe that **Jesus is keeping his promises** and that **the Holy Spirit has led and continues to lead** the Apostles and their successors into the fullness of the truth.

Why do Christians need the Church as well as the Bible?

For starters, Jesus *directly* gave us the Church, and only through the Church did He give us the Bible. If Christ had wanted a religion *just* of the book, He would have written it. But He didn't. Instead He established a living Church which He continues to lead through the Holy Spirit. It hardly makes sense to say that we can do without what Christ plainly thought was more important. By the way, God used the same process in the Old Covenant: First He formed his people which we can rightly call the Church of the Old Covenant, and out of this people He called Moses, the prophets, and certain others to commit his teaching to writing.

Second, it is clear to any observant person that the Bible is not self-interpreting. The great number of contradictory interpretations which have marked the many divisions of Protestantism makes that statement all too evident.

17

Third, those who believe that all we need is the Bible cannot find a biblical basis for that belief. Certainly the Bible says that "All Scripture is inspired by God and profitable for teaching, for reproof, for correction, and for training in righteousness" (2Tim 3:16), but just as certainly nowhere does it say that *only* Scripture constitutes the rule of faith and morals. In fact, the Bible itself says that the *Church* is the "pillar and bulwark of the truth (1Tim 3:15). Furthermore, St. Paul, who wrote so much of the New Testament, specifically calls attention to the role of Tradition — that which is handed down by verbal teaching and practice (1Cor 11:2, 23).

Why do we need the Church telling us what to do?

In reality, the above question really asks, "Why do we need Christ telling us what to do?"

The first thing that needs to be said is that Christ through his Church actually tells us to do very little that is specific. By that I mean that the Great Commandment to love each other as Christ has loved us does not tell us specifically what to do. This was mentioned above where we reviewed the Six Precepts of the Church.

However, in any age our human weaknesses need to be rebuffed and we need to hear again and again the challenge of keeping the Commandments, of not doing those things which God has revealed as wrong.

Isn't the Church hung up on sex today?

The Church is always "hung up" on love. Jesus came to teach us the truth about love, and He continues to teach those truths today. In an age in which sex is grossly misused, the Church is obliged to keep restating the demanding truth about love.

It is *Western culture* which is truly hung up on sex as is evident from the vast pornography industry and the ever increasing explicitness in the public media, thinly veiled advertising for prostitution (massage parlors and escort services), the use of sex as a primary marketing tool and the increasing acceptance of homosexual and lesbian sex. The sad effects are everywhere, frequently making the headlines: rapes, sexual murders, unfettered divorce and desertion, horrendous rates of out-of-wedlock pregnancies, epidemic levels of sexually transmitted diseases including the deadly AIDS, the sexual abuse of children and the killing of over one and one-half million unborn babies each year just in the United States. What was once universally considered a tragic necessity, the illegitimate child being raised by a single mother, is now being advocated as a perfectly acceptable lifestyle, deliberately planned and chosen. Lesbians make no secret of using artificial insemination to get themselves pregnant so they can raise children according to their false ideas and without the influence of a male presence in the house.

In this culture, the voice of Christ continuing to teach the timeless truths about the demands of love through his Church is clearly necessary and will certainly be counter-cultural! However, in the long view of history, the only criticism will be that the Church at the grass roots level did not speak up more loudly and frequently.

Why does the Church command us to worship at Mass every Sunday?

This precept or commandment of the Church derives directly from the Third Commandment: Keep holy the Sabbath Day. Since Jesus rose from the dead on the first day of the week, the Church of the New Covenant has kept Sunday as the Sabbath—a day of worship.

It is necessary to keep firmly in mind that the Commandments were given us for our benefit, and this is true likewise of the Third Commandment. As Jesus taught, "The sabbath was made for man, not man for the sabbath" (Mk 2:27). In other words, we have an inner need to worship God in spirit and in truth, and we need a day of rest. We need to worship God in the way He has given us, the holy sacrifice of the Mass, each week. To refuse to do so is to state to ourselves and to God that other things are more important. How does one explain that to God on judgment day?

Keeping Sunday holy involves more than attending Mass. It should also be a family day and a day of rest, not an ordinary work day. Sunday should not be a shopping day unless necessary to pick up a small item of food, preferably at a neighborhood mom and pop store. This was widely recognized in the United States until recently by Christian-influenced "blue laws" against regular commerce on Sundays, and Christians can and should still witness to the Sunday rest by not shopping on Sundays. (And when "A" shops, "B" has to work.) The laws of the Lord are for our own benefit.

Is it sufficient just to believe in Jesus and ignore all the rest?

Let's put it this way: is it sufficient just to hang your marriage license on the wall as proof of your love and to ignore your spouse?

We cannot overemphasize the importance of the feast of Christ the King on the last Sunday of the Church year, just before the first Sunday of Advent. This feast day reminds us that Jesus wants to be the King and Center of our personal lives. This is a never-ending challenge to most of us because of our tendencies to center our lives on ourselves. If we want to be with the Lord and to praise Him as King for all eternity, the time to start is now. Daily prayer, Sunday Mass, keeping all the commandments, and being of service to others are ways of doing so.

How does an adult Catholic learn more about the Catholic Faith?

There are a number of good books and tapes available for your further instruction. The *Catechism of the Catholic Church* (CCC) belongs in the library of every Catholic home. I also recommend *The Missionary's Catechism* by Russell L. Ford.[4] It's short, easy-to-read, and based on the CCC. As a guide for a lifetime of growth, I also recommend *The Catholic Lifetime Reading Plan* by Fr. John A. Hardon, S.J.[5]

In fact, there is a wealth of excellent material available today. Many proven treasures are being brought back into print, and with judicious selection of both new and old, every Catholic can become well informed. And being well informed is very important for bringing the truths of the faith to bear upon the very real problems that affect or afflict our society today.

Discuss with your fiance:

1. What did we learn from this chapter that is new to us or that we had forgotten?
2. Are we worshiping at Mass every Sunday? If not, why not, and how would I explain it to the Lord if I died tonight?

References

1. Clement of Rome, *Letter to the Corinthians*, circa A.D. 80, From William A. Jurgens, *The Faith of the Early Fathers, Vol. 1* (Collegeville, MN: Liturgical Press, 1970) p. 12. Jurgens thinks that the best evidence dates this letter at 80 A.D., not 96/98 as thought by some others. With either date, the point still holds. Clement, the successor of Peter at Rome, was writing as the supreme authority of the Church even while the Apostle John was still living.

2. St. Irenaeus of Lyons, *Adversus haereses,* (1, 10, 2) c. 190, quoted in W.A. Jurgens, *The Faith of the Early Fathers, Vol. 1,* (Collegeville, MN: Liturgical Press, 1970) p. 85.

3. St. Irenaeus of Lyons, (3, 3, 2) as above, p. 90.

4. Russell L. Ford, *The Missionary's Catechism* (Houston: Magnificat

Institute Press, 1998).

    5. John A. Hardon, S.J., *The Catholic Lifetime Reading Plan* (New York: Doubleday, 1989).

3. What Has to Happen for You to Marry?

You are planning to marry the one you love. You have undoubtedly talked much about *your* plans for marriage, but have you talked enough about *God's* plan for your marriage? You know that most Christians are called to work out their salvation in meeting the demands and fulfilling the responsibilities of married love, but how much have you discussed what those are? You know you have a special relationship with your beloved, but how much thought have you given to the *God-given* nature and permanence of that relationship? It is Almighty God who created the relationship of marriage, and this chapter will look at God's plan for you to grow in love through marriage.

The chapter title asks, "What has to happen for you to marry?" In other words, what conditions do each of you have to meet before you can enter a valid marriage? There may be a certain number of meetings and instructions that may be required in your diocese and parish, but those are not the concern of this chapter. Rather, our concern here might be better phrased, "What sort of understanding and commitment do you need to have in order to enter a true marriage?"

What do you do when you marry?

When you marry, you enter into a personal relationship of God's making. When you make your marriage vows, you make the contract of marriage and you also enter the covenant of marriage. A covenant involves far more than a contract. If you are both Christians, you enter the Sacrament of Matrimony. When you marry, you give yourself to your spouse and you obtain the moral right to engage in sexual intercourse, and you also have the responsibility to use sexual relations according to the plan of the Creator.

There's a lot of meaning in those sentences, so let us look at them in more detail.

What's meant by calling marriage a *personal* relationship?

First of all, marriage is a mutual relationship between two human persons. That may seem awfully obvious, but I emphasize "persons" to distinguish the marriage relationship from an emotional relationship. You can have an emotional but not a personal relationship with a pet dog or cat. Such animals have emotions, and many a breadwinner returning from work has been greeted more emotionally by the family dog than by his wife or children. In fact, there is sometimes an emotional bonding between a pet and its owner, but only a human person is capable of making the commitment of marriage. Furthermore, as the marriage ceremony teaches with the words "to have and to hold," you *possess* your spouse; however, you never *own* your spouse as a pet or a piece of property, something you can do with as you please.

This tells us something about the role of emotional attachment in marriage. It is usually very strong when you marry, but within marriage you can count on your emotional attachment varying from very strong to very weak. In fact, in a time of marital disillusionment, your emotional attraction to your spouse may be negative, but your bond of marriage endures.

The personal relationship of marriage far exceeds emotional feelings. It is based upon those spiritual characteristics that make us persons—intellect and will. That means that in order to enter the personal relationship of marriage, you have to have a basic understanding of what marriage is and you have to make a commitment of the will to enter it and to live it.

Marriage is a *mutual* personal relationship. Both you and your spouse must know what you are doing, and you must both make the marriage commitment.

"A personal relationship of God's making" — what does that mean?

The emphasis here is on *God's* role in your marriage.

You've probably heard it before but it's worth repeating: God made you to know Him, to love Him, and to serve Him in this life so that you can be with Him in heaven for all eternity.

God made your intended spouse for exactly the same reasons.

God created the relationship of marriage. He has inscribed the basic truths about marriage in our human nature; furthermore, knowing the darkness of our intellects and the weakness of our wills after the Fall of Adam and Eve, He has also revealed the truths about marriage through Jesus and his apostles.

God's plan for marriage is not arbitrary. That is, it isn't like a race with hurdles artificially placed here and there around the track. God's plan for marriage flows from our very nature which we have from Him. His plan is for our good.

"Personal" doesn't mean individualistic. We cannot—morally—create and live by our own ideas about marriage if they contradict God's plan for marriage. To do so is to contradict what it means to live as one created in the image and likeness of God and to contradict the meaning of Christian discipleship.

As a Christian, you are called to recognize that Jesus is the Lord, the King and Center of the universe. You must also recognize the dominion of the Lord over you and your marriage.

How important are tenderness and affection in marriage?

Very important. Pope John Paul II wrote that "tenderness and affection . . . constitute the inner soul of human sexuality in its physical dimension."[1]

That sounds so obvious that it may make no impression whatsoever at first. So put it in the context of the Sixties through the Eighties when the frequency of orgasm seemed to be the popular cultural criterion for marital "happiness." Put it also in the context in which the Pope was writing. Noting the vast difference between contraception and natural family planning, the Pope wrote as follows:

> To accept the cycle [of the wife] and to enter into dialogue means to recognize both the spiritual and corporal character of conjugal communion and to live personal love with its requirement of fidelity. *In this context* the couple comes to experience how conjugal communion is enriched with those values of tenderness and affection which constitute the inner soul of human sexuality in its physical dimension also.[2]

To put it another way, marital affection is so important that if there is none at all, even at the beginning of the marriage, such an absence would raise questions as to whether the couple had truly made the commitment of marriage. You need to keep in mind that the bedrock of your marriage covenant is love. A main characteristic of that love is that it is self-sacrificing in nature and other-centered. You must plan to give mutual help and service, based on love, in Christian marriage.

What is meant by calling marriage a contract?

The emphasis here is on the minimum essentials that are necessary for you and your intended spouse to enter a true marriage. These minimums are of two types: objective and subjective.

What are the objective "minimum essentials" about marriage?

You both must understand three things about marriage.
1. Marriage is permanent — "Until death do us part."
2. Marriage calls for fidelity although infidelity does not break the bond.
3. Marriage is for family.

What are the subjective minimum essentials for marriage?

There are four basic elements that each of you must possess and exercise in order for you to make the commitment of marriage:

1. You each have to be free to marry each other. This means that each of you are of sufficient age, that you are not married to anyone else, that you are of the opposite sex, and that you are not too closely related; i.e., you could not marry a close relative.

2. You have to have sufficient freedom to marry, and this refers to freedom from excessive outside pressures. Essentially that means that you aren't being forced to marry or under such pressure that it severely limits your freedom to make the yes-or-no decision about the proposed marriage.

3. You also need what the canon law of the Church calls "capacity." That means you are able to understand and fulfill the responsibilities of marriage. You might call this the inner freedom to marry. For example, if a person was a psychotic or had certain other severe psychiatric disorders, he or she would not have the psychological capacity to "commit marriage," i.e., to understand and make the commitment of marriage. In short, each of you has to "have it all together" sufficiently well in your own person before you can "commit marriage."

4. You both have to consent to what marriage really is. That's why it is so important for you to understand and believe what the Church teaches about marriage. It makes sense, doesn't it? To enter Christian marriage, you have to understand what you're getting into and consent to it.

Does that mean that anyone who isn't 100% normal can't make the commitment of marriage?

What human person is 100% normal? In the strictest sense, only Mary, the mother of Jesus. Conceived without Original Sin and sinless all her life. All the rest of us have our faults, foibles and sins which render us much less than perfect. These all too typical characteristics of us men and women do not modify our ability to "commit marriage"; probably 99% of us who are walking the streets and capable of earning a living are quite capable of understanding what marriage is all about and giving our consent.

What if only one of us agrees with the minimum essentials?

You must both make the commitment to marry according to God's plan—permanent, faithful, and for family. If only one of you makes the commitment, there's no true marriage. That's why it's so important for you to discuss these matters very early in your engagement; that's why it is so necessary for each of you to be honest when you are talking with the priest, deacon or other minister who is preparing you for marriage.

Can a person be forced to marry?

No. You must both marry freely. You cannot marry a person who is completely unwilling. "To marry freely" means that the old caricature of the shotgun wedding, "marrying" because the alternative was being murdered by vengeful relatives of a pregnant girl, was no marriage.

If we are pregnant now, should we tell the priest?

Yes. Definitely yes. He will want to know to what degree the pregnancy is your reason for getting married. Be honest with him. He doesn't want you unhappy, and he doesn't want one of you to come back in a few years saying that you were so pressured by the pregnancy that you weren't really free *not* to marry. If you feel that way now, get it out in the open. Don't make a mistake into a tragedy. You should be able to say honestly to yourself, to your spouse, to the priest, and to God that you would be marrying even if you were not pregnant.

What if I feel so strongly attracted to my fiance that I feel "almost forced" to marry?

To marry freely certainly doesn't mean that you are willy-nilly indifferent. It is normal to be strongly persuaded by your emotions and your intellect to make the commitment of marriage. How many people would ever get married without such attraction?

Can we hedge our bets and marry for better but not for worse?

No. That would act against the permanence of marriage. Marriage is a **God**-created relationship. Here's how the Second Vatican Council taught about marriage:

> The intimate partnership of married life and love has been established by the Creator and qualified by His laws. It is rooted in the conjugal covenant of irrevocable personal consent.[3]

This Council—a meeting of all the bishops of the Catholic Church—met in 1962-1965 to uphold and spell out what it means to be a Christian today. Obviously, the bishops are saying that to attempt to marry for better but not for worse would be an example of anti-Christian individualism; it would be a refusal to recognize God's dominion over each individual marriage.

What if a couple agree, before they marry, to end their marriage if "it's just not working out"?

If a couple would enter into such an arrangement, their union would not be a marriage, because marriage comes about not from the ceremony (necessary as that ordinarily is) but from "irrevocable personal consent." Such an arrangement would be a denial of the permanence of marriage.

In other words, you and your spouse will "commit marriage" by an act of your wills and by consummating that act of will by the act of marital intercourse which symbolizes your oneness in the Lord.

To enter an arrangement of living together without the true commitment of marriage is to fornicate—even if it has been preceded by a ceremony which would, of course, be fraudulent on the couple's part.

What is meant by calling marriage a covenant?

It means that the commitment of marriage is a *family* commitment: open-ended and unlimited. Compare a covenant to a contract. In a contract, you spell out all the details about what each party to the contract is obliged to do. If something isn't covered, it simply isn't covered and there is no contractual obligation. Furthermore, a contract will spell out the duration of the contract and how it can be ended, while the covenant of a true Christian marriage cannot be dissolved even by mutual consent.

The open-ended character of the marriage covenant is expressed in the traditional vows or promises of marriage: "for richer and for poorer, in sickness and in health, for better and for worse, until death do us part." It does not establish a "deal" but a *family*.

What is meant by calling marriage the Sacrament of Matrimony?

The Lord Jesus raised the natural state of marriage to the level of a sacrament. As you may remember from your basic catechism, a sacrament is a visible sign instituted by Christ to give sanctifying grace. Another way of saying it: the Seven Sacraments are actions of Christ by which He accomplishes at the supernatural level what the signs indicate at the natural level.

For example, the visible sign of the Sacrament of Baptism is the pouring of the water and the saying of the words. The sacrament uses the natural sign value of water which cleanses and sustains life. Through faith we know that in Baptism Jesus cleanses the soul from all sin and gives it supernatural life—the life of sanctifying grace. This is a created participation in the life of God Himself; it is the life of sanctifying grace which will enable you to live in the presence of God in heaven.

In the Sacrament of Matrimony the visible sign or action is the spoken exchange of the marriage vows. Through faith we know that this action creates more than just the natural bond of marriage, good as that is. Through faith we know that Jesus joins the Christian husband and wife into a supernatural and completely unbreakable relationship. Indeed, St. Paul concludes his teaching about marriage in his Letter to the Ephesians with this statement: "This is a great mystery, and I mean in reference to Christ and the Church" (Eph 5:32). (You can read the full text on the first page of Chapter 6 in this book.)

What are the practical and spiritual consequences of Matrimony being a Sacrament of Christ?

First of all, if we ask ourselves why a true Christian marriage is utterly unbreakable, it is because it is the symbol of the union of Christ and his Church; and that's a union that God has made unbreakable, no matter how sinful some in the Church may be. Note again the sentence from the Letter to the Ephesians just quoted in the above paragraph.

Second, if you are living in the state of sanctifying grace, the Sacrament of Matrimony increases God's gift of his life in you. In addition, your marital actions done under the promptings of the Spirit can further increase the life of grace within you. That means that your honest marital love-making as well as your sacrifices for each other can help you to grow spiritually as well as emotionally.

Third, the Sacrament of Matrimony brings with it an abundance of those promptings of the Holy Spirit called actual graces. These are the helps which will literally "enable" you to carry out God's will for you in marriage, to be patient and kind, to be thoughtful, and to improve your marriage. It is the workings of actual grace that will enable you to bring the sometimes unruly sexual drives or instincts under your control—or better, under the control of the Holy Spirit and at the service of true marital love.

In brief, when you resolve to live your marriage as God intends the Sacrament of Matrimony to be lived, He helps you abundantly to do so.

The flip side is this: If you decide not to live your marriage according to God's plan, then by sin you depart from the life of sanctifying grace. God will keep sending you his actual graces, calling you back, but the more you say no, the thicker you build the callous, and the harder it may be for you to return to the life of grace, without which no human person can live in heaven.

Why did God create the relationship of marriage?

The Second Vatican Council clearly teaches that God created matrimony for the raising of a family and the perfection of the spouses. "By their very nature, the institution of matrimony itself and conjugal love are ordained for the procreation and education of children, and find in them their ultimate crown."[4]

You and your spouse are called "to render mutual help and service to each other through an intimate union of their persons and of their actions."[5]

This "intimate union" of you and your spouse goes far beyond your physical unions. Indeed, you will find that you have to work at married love, for it requires much unselfishness.

> Such love, merging the human with divine, leads the spouses to a free and mutual gift of themselves, a gift proving itself by gentle affection and by deed. . . It far excels mere erotic inclination, which selfishly pursued, soon enough fades wretchedly away.[6]

To put it in very plain terms, God wants you and your spouse to grow in holiness. That's his purpose in creating you, and that's his *ultimate* purpose in joining you and your spouse in Holy Matrimony.

So, how important are children to Christian marriage?

Right now as you prepare for marriage, it is very possible that you have no idea how important the raising of a family is for you and your spouse. Vatican II teaches that while "marriage is not instituted solely for procreation," still, "marriage and conjugal love are by their nature ordained toward the begetting and education of children. Children are really the supreme gift of marriage and contribute very substantially to the welfare of their parents."[7]

Because the decision to have and to raise children in the ways of the Lord is implicit in the decision to marry, a decision before marriage never to have any children would normally render the proposed marriage completely null and void—no marriage at all. It would take an extremely serious reason such as a life or death risk to the mother's health to justify avoiding *completely* the responsibility of bearing and raising children, and, of course, such serious reason would justify only the use of natural family planning, not unnatural forms of birth control.

What if we are biologically unable to have children?

First of all, aside from perpetual impotency from the beginning of the marriage (which makes a man unable to consummate the marriage), a defect in nature which renders you unable to bear your own children does not affect the nature of your marriage bond: you are still married. The Fathers of Vatican Council II were quite clear about this: "Marriage persists as a whole manner and communion of life, and maintains its value and indissolubility, even when offspring are lacking—despite, rather often, the very intense desire of the couple."[8] We mention this because in some cultures husbands have divorced or deserted their wives because of the lack of children, and that's seriously wrong.

The second thing to note is that there are very definite moral limitations on what can be done to bear your own children. The end does not justify the means, and procedures which involve masturbation, "test-tube conceptions," micro-abortions, and the depersonalization of the marital act are morally wrong. We are all called to respect God's order of creation and his dominion over our lives.[9,10]

How do children "contribute very substantially to the welfare of their parents"?

The teaching of Sacred Scripture is still true: "Woman will be saved through bearing children if she continues in faith and love and holiness with modesty" (1 Tim 2:15). In addition, the raising of children helps parents to grow in the ways of love so prophetically described by St. Paul: "Love is patient and kind. . . is not jealous or boastful. . . is not irritable or resentful. . . hopes all things. . . endures all things" (1 Cor 13:4-7).

Look at it this way. The first two characteristics of love given by St. Paul are patience and kindness. Now, do you really think there is a better way for you and your spouse to develop the virtues of patience and kindness than in

31

being generous in raising children? It is part of God's plan for helping you to grow in holiness.

You will also find that as you and your spouse *both* exercise your roles of caring love toward your children, you will each grow in admiration and appreciation for the other, and your mutual love for each other will increase. In very plain speech, it is not at all unknown that a husband's efforts to help with the children and the responsibilities of the household are by far the biggest "turn-on" that he can provide for his wife that day or week.

Lastly, a modern writer with many years of experience in working with families has shared his insights by teaching that "children strengthen the *goodness* of the bond of marriage, so that it does not give way under the strains that follow on the inevitable wane or disappearance of effortless romantic love."[11]

What that means is that raising a family is part of your mission in marriage. God doesn't intend that marriage should just be an endless honeymoon, just the two of you gazing at each other and enjoying each other. *Deliberate* childlessness for an extended period of time can put a real strain on your relationship. Please listen well to the words of a priest with many years of experience dealing with families and in the Roman Rota—the highest court in the Catholic Church which has the final word on marriages which have failed.

> In my work at the Roman Rota, I not infrequently come across petitions of annulment of what clearly are perfectly genuine marriages of couples who married out of love, but whose marriages collapsed fundamentally because they deliberately delayed having children and thus deprived their married love of its natural support.
>
> If two people remain just looking ecstatically into each other's eyes, the defects that little by little they are going to discover there can eventually begin to appear intolerable. If they gradually learn to look *out* together at their children, they will still discover each other's defects, but they will have less time or reason to think them intolerable. They cannot, however, look out together at what is not there.
>
> Conjugal love, then, needs the support represented by children.[12]

In short, you marry to be friends in the **deepest** sense—to help each other on the path to heaven and to raise and educate children in the ways of the Lord. In turn, your children will help you as parents grow closer together and to God. Married love is for family, and family life with its combination of joys and sorrows is the ordinary way of working out your salvation.

Discuss with your fiance:

1. How is the marriage covenant different from a contract?

2. Since marriage is for family, can a couple, under normal circumstances, validly enter into marriage with the intention of never having children?

3. What does Vatican II mean when it teaches, "Children are really the supreme gift of marriage and contribute very substantially to the welfare of their parents"?

References

1. John Paul II, *Familiaris Consortio (The Apostolic Exhortation on the Family)*, 22 November 1981, n. 32.6.

2. Pope John Paul II, as above.

3. *The Documents of Vatican II*, Walter M. Abbott, S.J., ed. (New York: Herder and Herder, 1966) "Pastoral Constitution on the Church in the Modern World," n. 48. Hereafter "The Church Today."

4. *The Church Today*, n. 48.

5. *The Church Today*, n. 48.

6. *The Church Today*, n. 49.

7. *The Church Today*, n. 50.

8. *The Church Today*, n. 50.

9. Congregation for the Doctrine of the Faith, *Donum Vitae*, (Instruction on Respect for Human Life in Its Origin and on the Dignity of Procreation), 22 February 1987.

10. Sacred Congregation for the Doctrine of the Faith, *Declaration on Certain Questions Concerning Sexual Ethics*, 29 December 1975.

11. Cormac Burke, *Covenanted Happiness: Love and Commitment in Marriage* (San Francisco: Ignatius Press, 1990) 47.

12. Cormac Burke, 46-47.

4. "Until Death Do Us Part"

The last chapter focused on what has to happen within you in order for you to marry. This chapter focuses on what happens to you when you *do* marry. That is, "What really happens to each of you in the depth of your personhood when you marry?"

Marriage is intended by God to be a way in which husbands and wives grow in love and help each other and their children on the path to heaven. Yet in the United States, there is currently one divorce for every two marriages. No right thinking person can be happy about the horribly high divorce rate in the United States. Each divorce has its own history of unhappiness and sometimes tragedy, both for the parents and their children. Even unbelievers know that something is wrong in a culture with such a high rate of marital unhappiness and divorce.

The priest and others who are helping you to prepare for marriage know that at some time in the future you will have some difficulties which will test your commitment to remain married until death do you part. They do not want you to become a statistic. Indeed, they love you and want you to grow in Christian love and happiness. A prime reason you are asked to prepare well for marriage is to enjoy the true happiness that Christian marriage can bring.

You don't have to be a genius to recognize that many, many divorces stem simply from a lack of commitment by the spouses to keep their promises once the going gets tough. And you can easily see that if you think that you are morally free to remarry after a divorce, then it's much easier to weaken your commitment. Therefore, from a strictly practical viewpoint, you need to understand the unbreakable character of your marriage.

Lastly, but most important, as a Christian you will want to know what Jesus taught about marriage, and you need to follow his teaching.[1]

A word of caution. If your parents or other close relatives or friends are divorced, you may find a psychological obstacle to believing what Jesus teaches about divorce and remarriage. If this applies to you, it will be necessary to pray and to focus all the more strongly on who Jesus is—true God and true man, the Savior of the world, the Way, the Truth and the Life. Pray for such relatives and friends, but resist the temptation to water down the teaching of Jesus to fit the behavior you see around you.

35

What did Jesus teach about the permanence of marriage?

You find the teaching of Jesus about the permanence of marriage in four passages in the Gospels and in a letter of St. Paul.[2] The most concise passage comes from the Gospel of Luke.

> Every one who divorces his wife and marries another commits adultery, and he who marries a woman divorced from her husband commits adultery (Lk 16:18).

Did the Jews at the time of Jesus allow divorce and remarriage?

Divorce and remarriage were taken for granted among the Jews at the time of Jesus. However, there was a debate. The more conservative school of thought—the followers of Rabbi Shammai—believed that only a very serious reason could justify divorce; in practice that meant adultery or some other very serious moral misbehavior. The more liberal school—the followers of Rabbi Hillel—held that a man could divorce his wife for all sorts of reasons, even trivial ones. According to some, the liberal practice was the prevailing one.[3]

What did Jesus say about the Jewish divorce practices of his day?

Here is Matthew's account.

> Pharisees came up to Him and tested Him by asking, "Is it lawful to divorce one's wife for any cause?" He answered, "Have you not read that He who made them from the beginning made them male and female, and said, 'For this reason a man shall leave his father and mother and be joined to his wife, and the two shall become one'? So they are no longer two but one. What therefore God has joined together, let no man put asunder."
> They said to Him, "Why then did Moses command one to give a certificate of divorce and to put her away?" He said to them, "For your hardness of heart Moses allowed you to divorce your wives, but from the beginning it was not so. And I say to you: whoever divorces his wife, except for unchastity [in Greek, *porneia*, "indecency"], and marries another commits adultery, and he who marries a divorced woman commits adultery."
> The disciples said to Him, "If such is the case of a man with his wife, it is not expedient to marry" (Mt 19:3-10).

Matthew tells us that this wasn't just a simple, honest question; it was a test. The question was loaded: Could a man divorce his wife "for **any** cause" — as the liberal followers of Hillel taught? If Jesus said yes, then He could be criticized for laxity; if He said no, He could be accused of rigorism; at the least He would be accused of taking sides with one school or the other.

His answer caught everyone by surprise; He told them that they were both wrong; divorce was not possible for trivial reasons, and divorce was not possible even for serious reasons.

Jesus gave the most fundamental possible reason: quoting what the Jews recognized was the Word of God—the book of Genesis, He based his answer first upon the very **nature of man and woman** created in the image of God (Gen 1:27) and secondly upon the very **nature of marriage**—that the two become one flesh (Gen 2:24).

The response of the Jewish lawyers was immediate; like many lawyers, they looked for a precedent to justify their position, so they quoted Moses. Why did Moses command giving your wife a written certificate of divorce in order to put her away, they asked. Jesus told them plainly: "For your hardness of hearts. . ." And then He taught them about the fundamental law of God and the nature of marriage once again: "But from the beginning it was not so."

Actually, what Moses had done was to give at least some recognition of the rights of a woman not to be treated as a piece of property as was common in the Near Eastern world of his time. Prior to the dictate of Moses, a man could divorce his wife and then claim her back. With the written certificate of divorce, he gave up all future claim to her; at least she was no longer his yo-yo.

What about that phrase "except for unchastity"? Does that provide a reason for divorce with freedom to remarry in cases of infidelity, desertion, etc.?

No. If Jesus had meant that adultery and desertion were grounds for real divorce with the consequent freedom to remarry, He would have been siding with the conservative school of Shammai. But please notice well: He did not do that. He went back to Genesis, to the very order of creation. Look again at the last verse of Matthew's account. The teaching of Jesus was such a shocking surprise that the immediate reaction of his disciples was that if a man was really that "stuck" with his first wife, it would be better not to get married at all! His disciples clearly understood that He was not siding with the school of Shammai.

Second, making an exception for adultery and desertion would contradict the basic teaching of Jesus; it would have undermined his whole purpose in going back to the very order of creation. If adultery were grounds for divorce, all a man would have to do would be to have sex with someone he'd like for a new wife, and he would have broken free from the first marriage. Instead, Jesus spelled out very clearly that divorce and remarriage constitutes living in adultery. The Gospel of Mark makes this very clear:

> And in the house, the disciples asked Him again about this matter. And He said to them: "Whoever divorces his wife and marries another, commits adultery against her; and if she divorces her husband and marries another, she commits adultery" (Mk 10:10-12).

Third, the most likely meaning of "except for unchastity" is that it refers to marriages of close relatives which were condemned by Jewish law as indecent.[4] As indicated above, the Greek word translated as "unchastity" is *porneia* (pronounced por-nay-uh) from which we derive our word "pornography." So the phrase reads, "except for *porneia*— unions judged indecent because they had every appearance of incest."

What you need to realize is that the *porneia* clause does not offer any exception to the rule that true marriage is "until death do us part." Marriages judged to be incestuous, e.g., between a man and his stepmother (1 Cor 5:1) and between other close relatives, were acceptable in some societies long known to the Jews, but Jewish law condemned them as *porneia*. The early Christian Council of Jerusalem continued this condemnation (Acts 15:29). Therefore the clause "except for *porneia*" was no exception; it was a warning that no one, Jew or Greek, could enter into an incestuous union and expect the Church to recognize it. Such evil unions were not marriages; they both could and should be dissolved.

Are incestuous unions the only ones that can and should be dissolved?

No. While incestuous unions were apparently what Matthew was directly referring to when he wrote, any invalid marriage can and should be dissolved. For example, if a man and woman are living in adultery (one spouse still married before God to another person), such a union is immoral; it can and should be dissolved, or at least the couple should stop living together as man and wife.

What if abuse makes it impossible for two spouses to live together safely?

Under such circumstances, there can be a permanent separation "from bed and board." For reasons of child custody or financial independence, separated couples sometimes think it necessary to obtain a civil divorce. However, this does not dissolve the spiritual bond of marriage; civil divorce does not make the spouses morally free to marry someone else. As St. Paul taught: "To the married I give charge, not I but the Lord, that the wife should not separate from her husband (but if she does, let her remain single or else be reconciled to her husband) — and that the husband should not divorce his wife." (1 Cor 7:10-11).

What is meant by "indissolubility"?

"Indissolubility" is the technical word for the unbreakable character of a true marriage. It's a short way of saying that true Christian marriage cannot be dissolved, that marriage really is for keeps, "until death do us part."

This sounds very tough. What are the corresponding benefits of this permanence?

In the American culture in which fifty percent of first marriages and even higher percentages of second marriages end in divorce, the teaching of Jesus about the unbreakable bond of true marriage sounds hard indeed. You may well be thinking—or at least sympathizing—with those early disciples of Jesus when they first heard this teaching: if a man can't divorce his wife and remarry, maybe it's better not to marry (see Mt 19:10).

On the other hand, every thinking person knows that the American policy of unrestricted divorce and remarriage has wrought untold tragedy in the lives of individual families, frequently has devastating effects on the children as well as on one or both of the spouses, and has created tremendous problems for society at large. In its own perverse way, the American return to the wrongful marriage customs of the Jews at the time of Jesus has demonstrated the truth of his teaching.

What many today do not realize is that the idea of divorce and remarriage was glorified by many social liberals of the 1920s both in this country and in Europe. They called it "companionate marriage," and contraception played a key part in it. Marry, have marital relations, but be sure to use contraception; and when you get bored, divorce and remarry. Sound familiar? The big difference between then and now is that in the 1920s they were adding that if you had children, accidentally or on purpose, you should stay married for their benefit.

In 1930 Pope Pius XI responded to such attacks on marriage with an encyclical (a formal teaching letter) in which he pointed out five great benefits of indissoluble marriage.[5]

1. "Both husband and wife possess a **positive guarantee of the endurance** of this stability" which their very nature requires. In other words, by understanding that marriage is permanent and by freely making the commitment of marriage, each of you are guaranteeing to the other before God the enduring stability of your marriage. To understand this great benefit, contrast this true marital commitment with that of people entering modern, secularized "companionate marriage." In that case, neither spouse knows when the other may leave her or him for someone else. As a contemporary author has put it, in the current American scene, whoever wants out, wins.[6]

2. "A strong **bulwark** is set up in defense of a loyal chastity **against incitements to infidelity,** should any be encountered either from within or from without." What that means, I think, is that since you know deep in your heart that you cannot leave your spouse, you would have to face your spouse after any infidelity, and that realization can itself throw cold water on certain temptations. There's a new dimension today: an unfaithful spouse could very well contract a sexually transmitted disease, even AIDS, from a single act of infidelity, and then put his or her faithful spouse at risk, another very sobering thought.

3. "Any **anxious fear** lest in adversity or old age the other spouse would prove unfaithful **is precluded,** and in its place there reigns a calm sense of security." To marry is to pledge to each other that you want to grow old together.

4. Indissolubility is a great blessing **"in the training and education of children,** which must extend over a period of many years. . . since the grave and long enduring burdens of this office are best borne by the united efforts of the parents." Read any article about the effects of broken homes on the classroom, and you will recognize the wisdom of Jesus' teaching about the permanence of marriage.

5. Lastly there are **real benefits to society.** "Experience has taught that unassailable stability in matrimony is a fruitful source of virtuous life and of habits of integrity. Where this order of things obtains, the happiness and well-being of the nation is safely guarded; **what the families and individuals are, so also is the State."**

In the United States, we can add that the American experience demonstrates that one of the worst things our lawmakers have wrought upon this country is the "no-fault" divorce law which has contributed so much to the breakup of the American family and to many consequent social problems.

In summary, indissolubility is not a "rule of the Church." It is part of a loving Creator's plan. It is faithful to our true human nature, and its goodness should be clear:

> the good of a stable home or haven: of knowing that this "belongingness"—shared with others—is for keeps. People want that, are made for that, expect that it will require sacrifices and sense that the sacrifices are worth it. . . It is a strange head and heart that rejects the permanence of the marriage relationship.[7]

Can indissolubility affect your day-to-day marriage?

Yes, especially when the going gets tough. For example, what if you are angry with your spouse or simply depressed about your spouse's attitude or behavior? What sort of language will you use? If you know that you're going to be living together for the next 40 to 50 years, won't you watch what you say? Insults and cutting comments can still be causing a lot of hurt long after you've both forgotten what the original argument was all about. I'm not saying you have to be a doormat, but the permanence of your marriage is a very good reason to learn non-injurious ways of communication, and that's the purpose of Chapter 7 on communication.

Another example. Many men are very job-oriented, and many men lose their jobs—for whatever reasons. When a man loses his job, one of the few things he may have going for him some days is the quiet confidence that his wife will not be leaving him.

I'm sure you can think of other situations where the realization that you are together for life will affect your day-to-day marriage for the better. There's no doubt about it: God's revelation about the unbreakable permanence of true Christian marriage is a great blessing for Mankind.

What is an annulment?

The proper term is "declaration of nullity," and it is a judgment by a Church process that an "apparent marriage" was no marriage at all. Because the validity of a marriage is such a serious matter, the investigation leading up to a possible declaration of nullity often takes more than a year to complete.

If marriage is permanent, why is a declaration of nullity given?

It is granted because sometimes a couple enter an apparent marriage without "committing to marriage." One example was given in the preceding chapter—the mutual lack of commitment in "hedging their bets," and there are others. For example, one party might be serious about marriage, but the other person might, from the beginning, view the relationship simply as a social steppingstone to be ended when someone more useful turns up.

Then "annulments" aren't just a Catholic form of divorce with freedom to remarry?

Definitely not. Although there is the possibility that the application of certain grounds of nullity, especially psychological ones, can be abused, the point remains: there are some unions that utterly fail to meet the requirements of true marriage from the very beginning. This reality of non-marriage should be recognized, and such unions should be ended. Or, if possible, they should be rectified and reconsecrated.

What's the conclusion?

Do you remember the question at the beginning of this chapter? "What really happens to each of you in the depth of your personhood when you marry? Now we can answer that question.

When you marry, you and your spouse create a relationship that is part of your very personhood. In marriage, you and your spouse become one flesh. As husband and wife you create a relationship of oneness that is just as real and permanent as any blood relationship. A father may have disagreements with his son, even disown him, but he cannot cease to be his father. So also with husband and wife.

Jesus teaches us God's truth about human love. Jesus teaches us the demands of love that stem right from our nature as "made in the image and likeness of God" and from the very nature of marriage itself as created by God.

Therefore Jesus taught—and continues to teach—that Christian marriage is for keeps. No exceptions. It is permanent. There is no out. If horrible circumstances occur, it may be necessary for one spouse to leave the other for the safety of herself (or himself) and the children. But the couple's original bond created by their marriage vows before God still remains before God regardless of any civil laws, and neither party is free to remarry. Any attempt at such "remarriage" falls under the words of Jesus himself—it is adultery.

Discuss with your fiance:

1. Jesus taught us about the permanence of marriage; we are therefore not free to divorce and remarry. Is each of us ready and willing to make the commitment of Christian marriage?

2. What are the benefits of indissoluble marriage?

3. How will the realization of the permanence of your marriage affect your day-to-day living of marriage?

References

1. Portions of this chapter are adapted from *"Until death do us part"* (Cincinnati: Foundation for the Family, Inc., 1992).

2. Mt 5:31-32; Mt 19:9; Mk 10:11-12; Lk 16:18; 1 Cor 7:10-11.

3. E. Schillebeeckx, O.P., *Marriage: Human Reality and Saving Mystery* (New York: Sheed and Ward, 1965) 143.

4. John P. Meier, *The Vision of Matthew* (New York: Paulist Press, 1979) 248-257.

5. Pope Pius XI, *Casti Connubii* (Concerning Chaste Marriage), 31 December 1930. All references in this section are to paragraph 36.

6. Maggie Gallagher, *Enemies of Eros: How the sexual revolution is killing family, marriage and sex and what we can do about it* (Chicago: Bonus Books, Inc., 1989) 194. "What the divorce advocates never got into their heads is that some choices preclude others. If everyone can choose divorce, then no one can choose marriage . . . Men and women no longer have control over the terms of our marriages. We do not know what bargain we have struck getting married and it hardly matters since the culture and court will not enforce any bargain. The rule is: he who wants out, wins."

7. Burke, 44.

5. Marital Love and Sexuality

You are preparing for a lifetime of marital love. I hope (and you hope) that there will also be a lifetime of romance in your marriage, but married love is more than that. Married love is frequently called "conjugal love," and, of course, it involves sexuality. Let us take a look.

I.

What is conjugal love?

You can get a fair start at understanding married love by looking at the word "conjugal." It comes from the Latin word "conjugium" which literally means "with a yoke." And what's a yoke? The first definition in my dictionary describes it as a wooden bar which joins two animals so they can work together.

Obviously, there are many differences between that notion and marriage. For example, animals do not freely choose to enter such an arrangement. Still, there are two truths about marriage that are implicit in the term "conjugal" love. First of all, marriage does bind you and your spouse together, as the last chapter explained; this is also implied in another word for marriage—wedlock. Secondly, it is not an arbitrary binding because God does not give us moral norms as a whim, just to make life difficult. To the contrary, this being "locked into" marriage is for your mutual good—so that you and your spouse will work together for a lifetime.

Is such a notion compatible with Christian freedom?

Definitely yes. The Lord Jesus himself used the image of the yoke to describe Christian discipleship:

> Take my yoke upon you, and learn from Me; for I am gentle
> and lowly in heart, and you will find rest for your souls. For
> my yoke is easy, and my burden is light (Mt 11:29-30).

Jesus used the image of the yoke to describe how we are to be bound to Him for the purpose of achieving salvation. We are privileged to use the same image for the bonds of marriage in which you and your spouse will be bound — also for the purpose of working out your salvation together.

What are your marital rights?

The term "marital rights" generally refers to the right to engage in natural sexual intercourse. ("Natural" means intercourse which respects the way God has made our human *nature*. This includes both the way God has created the physical structure of the marital act and also the rights and dignity of one's self and one's spouse.)

St. Paul was asked about these matters by the Corinthian converts, some of whom had previously been involved in serious sexual sin and were now wondering if *any* sex was morally permissible. So the Apostle Paul wrote:

> Now concerning the matters about which you wrote. It is well for a man not to touch a woman. But because of the temptation to immorality, each man should have his own wife and each woman her own husband. The husband should give to his wife her conjugal rights, and likewise the wife to her husband. For the wife does not rule over her own body, but the husband does; likewise the husband does not rule over his own body, but the wife does. Do not refuse one another except perhaps by agreement for a season, that you may devote yourselves to prayer; but then come together again, lest Satan tempt you through lack of self-control. I say this by way of concession, not of command (1 Cor 7:1-6).

Are there other marital rights?

Certainly. However, it can sometimes be confusing or misleading to list your various marital rights without at the same time mentioning your corresponding responsibilities, so let us look at some areas of matching rights and responsibilities.

Sexual matters. First of all, you are a human person, and you have the right to be respected by others, including your spouse. Each of you has the right to be treated with respect by the other, and both you and your spouse have the duty or responsibility to treat each other with respect. Big problems have developed in some marriages because one spouse wrongly interpreted the above passage of Sacred Scripture to mean absolute ownership of his or her spouse without regard to the conscience and feelings of the spouse.

Specifically, having rights to marital relations does not mean that you have the right to do anything and everything imaginable to or with your spouse. The principle of respect means that your sexual activities must not only be morally permissible but they must also be mutually acceptable. Take oral-genital contact, for example. While such contact is not condemned when it is part of foreplay to completed genital-genital marital relations, it may not be forced upon an unwilling spouse. And "forced" does not refer just to physical force; pouting, door slamming, the silent treatment, being generally nasty are all ways of trying to force a spouse to do something he or she does not want to do.

As mentioned above, once married, you each will have a right to normal marital relations. The law of the Church for ages has spelled this out: each spouse has a right to those acts which of their very nature are ordered toward the procreation of children. This means that you will also have a corresponding duty not to refuse the reasonable request of your spouse for honest marital relations. (So don't use sex as a weapon.) It means further that each of you has the duty of making such activity true acts of marital love, acts which can honestly symbolize the self-giving and caring love you pledge when you marry. More on that in the next chapter.

The right to normal and honest marital relations also means that no one has a right to contraceptive behaviors. Such behaviors include intercourse with barrier contraceptives, the Pill or Norplant or other chemical birth control, the IUD, fellatio, cunnilingus, mutual or solitary masturbation, or marital sodomy whether anal or oral, and sexually sterilized intercourse.[1] Confusion about these matters and lack of agreement to avoid these practices has led to tremendous problems within some marriages, even to divorce. It would not be surprising if you found it quite unpleasant, to say the least, to discuss some of these matters. But do yourself a favor: at least ask your fiance if he or she agrees with everything in this chapter. If he or she doesn't, then you had better find out now what your differences are because the contraceptive behaviors mentioned above are a serious moral matter; they are incompatible with authentic Christian discipleship no matter how common they may be in an age which takes sexual immorality for granted. For a person to know this moral seriousness and nonetheless deliberately pursue such acts is to commit mortal sin—sin which breaks one's bonds with both Christ and his Church.

Religion. You have the right and the duty to pray to God in true worship at Sunday Mass every week; you have the right and duty to pray daily. It may seem awkward at first, but it will be very good for the two of you to pray together out loud, even if it's no more than a bedtime Hail Mary for yourselves and for each one of your children. If that seems too much at first, perhaps you could start with a minute or so of mutual silent prayer. I highly recommend praying a daily rosary together, for the daily rosary was the

47

request of Our Lady in her apparitions at Fatima. If you allow your marriage to become secularized, (i.e., a thing merely of this earthly life) you will definitely lose something very positive in this life, and you may regret it for all eternity.

Your personal relationship. You have the right to feel loved and appreciated by your spouse, and you have the corresponding duty to help your spouse feel loved and appreciated by you. This may sound superfluous to you as you prepare for marriage and have wonderful feelings about each other. However, one of the greatest problems in marriage is that of feeling unloved and unappreciated. Where is the spouse who hasn't at some point felt taken for granted? And where is the spouse who hasn't at some time taken his or her spouse for granted? It is an almost universal challenge. As indicated in Chapter 3, the thoughtless failure of a spouse to fulfill his or her responsibilities in this regard does not affect the nature of the marriage bond, but it can provide unnecessary sources of temptation.

This is not a book of helpful hints on how to get along in marriage, but one thing can be said in general: it's the little things that count—as refreshing as a glass of cold water on a hot day or as irritating as sand in your shoes on a long walk.

Your children. Within marriage, you have a God-given right to seek to bear children and raise a family; you have a corresponding duty to have children and to raise them in the ways of the Lord. (No one has an absolute right to bear children, for children are gifts from the Lord, not property which can be owned.) Such rights and duties also include the right and obligation to try to determine how many children God wants you to have and the corresponding duty to be generous to the Lord in accepting children. More about this in Chapter 8.

Your big enemies here are widespread public opinion that two children are enough and a pervasive materialism that urges you to think more in terms of comfortable lifestyles than of Christian discipleship. So ask yourselves: "What if God gives us a third or a fourth child? What if God doesn't give us any children? What if God gives us a special child who needs extra care?" I suggest you need to pray for the grace to be as generous as God calls you to be; you certainly need his help to run counter to an anti-Christian culture in which children are too often viewed as impediments to a lifestyle of greater convenience.

Society. You have a right to support from society, and you have a matching right and duty to make a contribution to the common good of society. You have a right to tax laws which realistically recognize the costs of raising a family and which favor those who are doing the most important job in any society—raising the next generation in the ways of the Lord. You have a duty to raise your children to respect the rights of God and man and the just laws of their country. You have a right to the moral support of the community in raising a family, and you may have a duty, depending upon the talents the Lord has given you, to raise your voice and even take political action to help create that support.

Education. You and your spouse will be called by God to be the primary educators of your children. The basic human right to educate your children belongs to you, not to any school system whether public or private. It is also your responsibility to educate your children— primarily in the ways of the Lord but also in the skills necessary for earning a living and making a contribution to society. You may delegate part of this responsibility to a school, but the primary right and responsibility remains yours. As your children approach school age and as you become more aware of education in these United States, you may come to understand why more and more parents—from doctors to laborers—each year decide that they can best fulfill their educational responsibilities by teaching their children at home.

Is there a recipe for marital love and happiness?

Marriage counselors write dozens of marriage recipe books, some of them very good, and yet the American divorce rate stays outrageously high. I think it's best to turn to Sacred Scripture, where you will find—in various places—the ingredients for a biblical recipe for marital love and happiness. Start with the famous text of St. Paul dealing with love (1 Cor 13:4-7). Older translations used the word "charity," but the use of "love" helps us to understand its application to the people we are closest to—spouse and family.

> Love is patient and kind;
> love is not jealous or boastful;
> it is not arrogant or rude.
> Love does not insist on its own way;
> it is not irritable or resentful;
> it does not rejoice at wrong, but rejoices in the right.
> Love bears all things, believes all things, hopes all things, endures
>   all things.

To get the full effect of that, try this paraphrase:
> I will be patient and kind with my spouse;
> I will not be jealous or boastful;
> I will not be arrogant or rude;
> I will not insist on my own way;
> I will not be irritable or resentful;
> I will not rejoice at my spouse's wrongdoing or mistakes but will rejoice in the right—and especially the good that my spouse does.
> I will bear all things, believe all things, hope all things, endure all things—especially my personal daily cross.

What a tremendous challenge!

If you and your spouse make a monthly confession and use this as a starter for an examination of conscience, you will certainly be on the right track for a marriage of lasting love and happiness.

Other parts of the biblical recipe for marital love and happiness will be given in the following chapters.

II.

What is the meaning of sexual intercourse?

Sexual intercourse is intended by God to be *at least implicitly* a renewal of a couple's marriage covenant. Some might think that statement goes beyond the formal teaching of the Catholic Church, but it is entirely in accord with it and helps to explain it.

What is meant by "at least implicitly"?

The phrase "at least implicitly" means two things. First of all, you don't have to have explicitly in mind that your marital relations are meant to be a renewal of your marriage covenant. You don't need to invite your spouse to the marriage act by saying, "Come, let us renew and reaffirm our marriage covenant." However, you will find it helpful for your overall marriage and for your marital relations never to forget this very real meaning—this covenant meaning—of sexual intercourse.

Second, that phrase "at least implicitly" means that you cannot morally act explicitly against your marriage covenant. The most obvious example of that would be spouse swapping which is simply mutually agreed upon adultery. (Yes, it does happen, weird as it may seem.) The forcing of sex against the legitimate wishes of your spouse would be another obvious example of acting against the caring love of your marriage covenant.

What is the symbolism of marital relations?

When you marry, you vow to give yourself without reservation to your spouse. You vow your fidelity; you pledge that you will exercise caring love towards your spouse "until death do us part." You and your spouse create a oneness that the Bible speaks of as becoming "two in one flesh."

Once you are married, you and your spouse are privileged to celebrate the oneness you and God have created with the two-in-one-flesh act of marital intercourse. Your marital relations symbolize your commitment and the oneness of your marriage relationship. In fact, one of the purposes of marital relations is to further cement your relationship, to increase your mutual bonding and love for each other.

What is the marital meaning of sex?

First of all, Sacred Scripture teaches that sexual intercourse is intended by God to be a **marriage act.** The Bible makes this clear by condemning all the other forms of sex — in alphabetical order, adultery, bestiality, contraception, fornication, masturbation and sodomy. All that is left is honest sexual intercourse by a married couple—a true marriage act.

Second, marital relations should reflect the caring love pledged by the couple at marriage.

Sometimes people speak about "social intercourse." What's the connection between this and sexual intercourse?

The real "love making" occurs in "social intercourse," i.e., the mutual help that spouses give to each other in the kitchen, conversation in the living room, helping with the children, cleaning up the yard, etc. Your social intercourse should reflect the sacrifices and the caring love you pledge at marriage, and that is the great challenge of marriage. Then your marital relations will be a reflection of your day to day love, not a contradiction to daily indifference.

How can an act of such great pleasure be an act of self-giving?

This question reflects the need to see marital relations as a marriage act. It is at marriage that you and your spouse will make the great gift of self to each other. The more you understand about marriage, the more you will come to appreciate the self-giving nature of your marriage commitment. Therefore, to the extent that your total marriage reflects the self-giving love you pledged at your wedding, to that extent your acts of marital relations will be truly an honest symbol of your marriage covenant and truly acts of self-giving love.

What if we are having pre-marital sex?

The only Christian answer is, "Stop!" To repeat, sexual relations are intended by God to be at least implicitly a renewal of your marriage covenant. Therefore, sex before or outside of marriage is essentially dishonest; it is a lie. It pretends to be what it cannot be. An engaged couple is no more married and privileged to have sexual intercourse than a deacon is ordained and privileged to celebrate Mass. In both cases, each person has to wait for marriage and ordination respectively.

Waiting until marriage is not just a "Church rule." It is not waiting for the Church to give you "permission" to have sexual relations. Instead, the waiting is for *you*. Sexual intercourse is intended by God to be a marriage act, and you are not morally and spiritually equipped to engage in the marriage act until you are married.

In addition, having sex even occasionally before marriage is a bad way to prepare for marriage. Engagement is a time to raise the level of your spiritual intimacy by "exploring and sharing ideas, goals, dreams and hopes, values, [and] problems."[2]

Worse yet is the make-believe world of "living together as man and wife" before you are married. First of all, it truly is "living in sin," and that's all any Christian should need to know. Second, it is unrealistic because each party knows that the other can leave at any moment without a trace of legal or marital obligation; so one person or the other or both may try to be just too nice, all the while building up resentment and waiting to really "be herself or himself" once they have made the public commitment of marriage.

Finally, living together just doesn't work as a preparation for marriage. Research has shown much higher divorce rates for couples who live together before marriage.[3]

Engagement is a time to get to know your fiance and to let yourself be known. I'm not advocating a recital of all your past sins. However, if your mom or dad or your siblings have been telling you for years that you are too self-centered, too impatient, too hard driving or too lazy, too critical of yourself or others, etc., maybe you should be discussing with your fiance how he or she can help you to improve in these areas without falling into nagging.

As mentioned above, engagement is a time to share ideas, and that includes finding out and disclosing to each other what each of you reads. If one of you is reading *Playboy* or other forms of pornographic material, you have a problem now and the potential for a huge problem later on. The annual swimsuit edition of *Sports Illustrated* is not harmless; it has nothing to do with a healthy interest in sports; it has everything to do with encouraging men to view women as sex objects and to engage in unrealistic fantasies about what women should look like, etc.

What if, as our marriage matures, we find that there's quite a difference in our interest in sexual relations?

That means that the honeymoon is over and that you are part of the vast majority of the human race. It is common for one spouse, typically the wife but not always, to have less interest in having marital relations. In fact, based on the wide difference between the sexual desires of many husbands and the desires of their respective wives, I have concluded that God has a sense of humor.

Sometimes husbands have an unrealistic expectation of what to expect from a loving wife. Such husbands may think that the modern television and movie portrayal of women as aggressive sex kittens is based on real life. While I'm sure there are some or many exceptions, the big majority of women are not naturally aggressive about sex.

In early 1985 Ann Landers asked her women readers, most of whom (as typical Americans) practice contraception: "Would you be content to be held close and treated tenderly, and forget about 'the act'? Answer yes or no and please add one sentence: I am over (or under) 40 years of age." Of 90,000 responses, 72% said "yes" to cuddle-only, and 40% of those were under 40. It was hardly a scientific study, but it gives a rough idea about widespread differences in interest in sex.

In certain cases, part of this difference may stem from feelings of being used, and thus it is not surprising that this feeling appears to be less prevalent among couples practicing natural family planning than among contraceptors. In response to the Ann Landers' survey, the Couple to Couple League for Natural Family Planning promptly surveyed its membership with the same question, and only 8.4% of wives responded "yes."

Some difference in sexual interest is normal. The practices of periodic abstinence and marital courtship generally keep this difference from becoming large enough to pose a problem.

Discuss with your fiance:

1. Do we accept Catholic teaching regarding love and sexual behavior? If not, why not?

2. Since sexual intercourse is intended by God to be at least implicitly a renewal of the marriage covenant, what conclusion can be drawn about sex outside of marriage?

3. How does real "making love" occur in a couple's everyday activities such as raising children, conversations, household help, etc.?

4. We have the right and duty to pray daily. Am I willing to pray aloud together with my spouse? If I'm not, why not?

References
  1. For further explanation of permissible sexual behaviors, see the leaflet, "Marital Sexuality: Moral Considerations," Couple to Couple League, P.O. Box 111184, Cincinnati, OH 45211. Single copy: free with SASE.

  2. Pat Driscoll, "A Letter to a Friend," *CCL Family Foundations,* March-April 1992, p. 20.

  3. "Living together risks love. Study: Divorce more likely," *Cincinnati Enquirer*, 3 September 1992, p. A-7. Article refers to a study published in the August issue of *Demography* whose authors refer to other studies showing that "couples who live together before marriage have divorce rates 50% to 100% higher than those who don't."

6. In Marriage, Who's the Boss?

In marriage, that's the wrong question. In fact, if that's a real question for you as you prepare for marriage, you may be heading for trouble. However, to say that "Who's the boss" is the wrong question is not the same as saying there is no divinely established authority within marriage. There is, and it's called headship.

Has God entrusted the role of headship in the family to either one of the spouses?

Yes. However, as you will see in the following passage, headship is a far cry from "bossism." The famous text dealing with this question is found in the Letter of St. Paul to the Ephesians and is part of the biblical recipe for marital happiness. Note well the very first verse.

> [21]Be subject to one another out of reverence for Christ. [22]Wives, be subject to your husbands, as to the Lord. [23]For the husband is the head of the wife as Christ is the head of the Church, his body, and is Himself its Savior. [24]As the Church is subject to Christ, so let wives also be subject in everything to their husbands.
>
> [25]Husbands, love your wives, as Christ loved the church and gave himself up for her, [26]that He might sanctify her, having cleansed her by the washing of water with the word, [27]that He might present the Church to Himself in splendor, without spot or wrinkle or any such thing, that she might be holy and without blemish. [28]Even so husbands should love their wives as their own bodies. He who loves his wife loves himself. [29]For no man ever hates his own flesh, but nourishes and cherishes it, as Christ does the Church, [30]because we are members of his body.
>
> [31]"For this reason a man shall leave his father and mother and be joined to his wife, and the two shall become one." [32]This is a great mystery, and I mean in reference to Christ and the Church; [33]however, let each one of you love his wife as himself, and let the wife see that she respects her husband (Eph. 5:21-33).

In verse 21, St. Paul prepares us for what follows. Though he will have to teach the headship role of the husband, he first puts it in the context of mutual submission to each other. This reminds us of the teaching of Jesus that among his disciples, leadership means service, not lording it over someone else (Lk 22:24-27), and of his action at the Last Supper when He washed the feet of his disciples (Jn 13:3-17).

Future wives, in verse 22, St. Paul gives what may be one of your greatest challenges as a modern wife—the command to be subject to your husband. Note, however, how the Apostle qualifies it: "as to the Lord." Now what the Lord wants is what is truly for your good, and the Lord never asks you to do anything sinful. So if your husband asks or demands that you use the Pill or some other unnatural form of birth control or wants you to engage in other immoral sexual activities, then he has strayed far from his role of headship; and, of course, that holds true for any form of immorality, not just sexual sins.

Future husbands, note well the great challenge of verse 25, the command to love your wife as Christ loved the Church and gave Himself up for her. Complete self-giving love. It means dying to self in order to be helpful to your wife, even that you might help sanctify her, that is, that you might help her to grow in holiness. No grounds for bossism here!

If headship doesn't mean "boss," then what does it mean?

Headship means leadership. Headship means accepting and carrying out the responsibility of family leadership in the things that count for eternity as well as in matters of day to day living such as supporting your family. For example, family prayer and worship; bringing up your children in the ways of the Lord both by word and by example.

One of the great problems of the modern Western family has been the widespread abdication of husband leadership. Too many husbands are giving the impression to their children that what counts in life is money and sports, or sports and money. As the children get older, they get another message: add sex to money and sports; women are to be the playthings of men. Authentic religion — responding to God on his terms, real Christian discipleship — well, that's for the wife. As a result, many young people are growing up without any sort of image of a man who takes seriously the important things in life.

How can husbands be encouraged to fulfill their responsibilities of headship?

The old saying that behind every successful man there stands a supporting wife holds true here as well. It starts with courtship and engagement. A woman can help a man to understand the importance of living according to God's law; she can expect—indeed, demand—respect both for herself and for keeping the Commandments. Her example of accepting the Lordship of Christ will encourage him to do so also.

Does husband-headship imply that men are superior to women? Or that women are morally or spiritually unequal to men?

Not at all. In fact, sociological data indicate that women are generally more competent in many areas that really count in life such as building relationships in the family, etc. Aside from physical strength, perhaps it is true that men are the weaker sex. If so, then God's appointment of husbands to headship is right in line with his pattern of choosing the weak things of the world to accomplish his works (1Cor 1:26-30).

Pope John Paul II has spoken about the mystery of order within equality:

> It can be said that in Paul's thought married love comes under a law of equality, which man and woman fulfill in Jesus Christ (cf. 1 Cor 7:4). However, when the Apostle observes: "The husband is head of his wife just as Christ is head of the Church, He himself the Savior of the body" (Eph 5:23), the equality, the interhuman parity, is surpassed because there is order within love. The husband's love for his wife is a participation in Christ's love for the Church . . . This relationship between Head and Body does not cancel marital reciprocity, but rather strengthens it.[1]

In brief, the Pope recognizes the marital headship of the husband, calling it "order within love;" the spouses are otherwise equals as noted above. Recognizing this and living it takes the grace of Christ.

But isn't husband headship sexist and out of date?

No. It is not based on any alleged superiority of men; it is based simply and solely on the spiritual principle that as Christ is the head of his family the Church, so a husband is to be the head of his family.

The biblical principle from St. Paul doesn't go out of date. *Someone* has to be the head, just as in the Church where Christ chose 12 Apostles and made one of them the head. If you reject the biblical, spiritual basis for headship, what other lasting basis do you have? Test scores? Physical power? Ability to talk the fastest or the loudest?

I suspect that some young women will have trouble with this. It goes against the grain of a certain feminism (as contrasted with femininity) that pervades the late 20th Century and which disregards the real differences between men and women. To such women I offer this counsel: out of love for your husband, accept and respect the biblical, spiritual principle of husband headship.

First of all, you will benefit spiritually by doing so.

Second, it may be the best way for you to encourage your husband to truly accept a Christian leadership role in your family.

Third, by accepting husband headship, you help to establish the importance of living your marriage by religious principles. The time will most likely come in your marriage, whether at five or more than 25 years, when marital disillusionment will set in. The *feelings* of love are temporarily gone. Your husband may be thinking that marriage with you will be another 20 to 40 or more years of purgatory. At such times, his staying around to work through this unhappy experience may depend mostly upon his conviction about the importance of conforming to religious principles—in that case that he is bound before God by your mutual marriage vows and really has no other morally decent choice.

If husbands and wives are to "be subject to one another" (v.21), what do they do if they simply cannot agree about something?

When husband and wife take seriously their responsibilities as spouses and parents in the light of Christian discipleship, and when they strive to be mutually submissive to each other in Christ, the areas of serious disagreement will be very few indeed. However, the time may come when there is an honest difference that cannot be reconciled or compromised: a decision has to be made to do one thing that excludes the other. Perhaps he has no choice about his vacation time and he believes that as a family they should visit his aging parents who are in poor health; the problem is that by doing so, the children will miss an important swimming meet, and the wife wants them in that competition. He makes the decision as the head of the family that they will do an act of mercy by visiting the parents. (If you don't like the example, make up your own.) The point is that attitude is all important.

His should be one of regret for any disappointment or pain caused by his decision, never one of victory. Hers should be one of acceptance, of offering it up, never one of resentment and moodiness.

Of great importance, no matter *whose* opinion a couple decide to follow, they ought to present a united front to their children. It needs to be, "Your father and I (or your mother and I) have decided . . ."

Wouldn't it be best to ignore this headship thing since we plan to agree on everything that's important?

If you plan to agree on everything that's important, then start by agreeing on the role of husband headship. How can we call something unimportant when it is specifically called for in Sacred Scripture?

Perhaps Scripture is revealing to us that a husband has a very real psychological need for headship, a real need for respect within the confines of his own family. At work, he may be subject to bosses who make him feel much less than a man; or he may be the "boss" and know that no matter what he does, he is subject to the behind-the-back, carping criticism of his subordinates. Perhaps Scripture is revealing to us that wives have a real psychological need to be submissive to the one to whom they have pledged their lifelong love and fidelity. Perhaps Scripture is revealing that these needs are complementary, that a husband needs a wife who will build him up, help him to feel like a man, i.e., to help him to grow in healthy self-respect, help him to accept his responsibilities as head of the family. Perhaps Scripture is revealing that a wife will find some of her greatest joys in helping her husband in these ways.

Let me put it this way. When a mother breastfeeds her baby, the hormone prolactin increases dramatically and helps her to feel more motherly; the hormone helps her to accept more easily the responsibilities of motherhood. Perhaps if a husband is helped by his wife to feel that he really is the head of the family, he will more easily accept the responsibilities that go along with headship; perhaps he will more easily exercise caring and patient love to his wife and to his children; perhaps he will more readily overlook *his* fatigue and be attentive to hers.

Discuss with your fiance:

1. Sacred Scripture compares the relationship between husband and wife to the relationship between Christ and his "bride," the Church. What does this teach us about the marital relationship?

2. Headship or family leadership means accepting responsibilities in areas that really count — spiritual areas as well as day to day matters. What are some of those specific areas?

3. Many events, sporting and others, are scheduled on traditional family days such as Thanksgiving, Christmas, and Sundays. If you believe that family life is important, how will you put that conviction into practice in the face of such events?

References
   1. "Christ loves his Bride, the Church," *L'Osservatore Romano*, weekly English edition, 18 December 1991.

7. Communication

Volumes have been written in recent years about the importance and the techniques of communication. There is no question: *how* you communicate with your spouse and *what* you communicate to your spouse will have a great influence on your marital happiness. You might say, "Well, couples lived peaceful, stable marriages for centuries before the current focus on good communication between spouses so why all the current fuss?" That's true, but the social pressures upon you to let your marriage disintegrate are much greater than they were for many of those centuries, so it is probably much more important for you to put real effort into your marital communication.

This chapter is written from the perspective that you are already married, but reading it while you're engaged may also be helpful; it may help you to realize that every married couple has to work both as individuals and as a couple to keep their relationship civil and happy.

How do spouses communicate?

Spouses communicate the same way everyone does — verbally and with body language. Frequently these are not separate. For example, if you say the words "Thank you," your tone of voice can communicate that you are genuinely grateful for something. On the other hand, the same words said with sarcasm and shouted at top volume would communicate something entirely different. Is that pure verbal communication or is it verbal plus body language? I'm not trying to open or close a debate; I use the illustration simply to indicate how mixed these two aspects are in much of our communication.

What should we communicate about?

Almost anything. American social convention frowns on politics, religion, and sex as topics of casual conversation with strangers at a dinner party, thus leaving you largely with jobs, sports, the weather, and current events. Certainly, however, religion and sex are important topics within a marriage. For starters, why not discuss well the chapters of this book?

Minds empty? Why not develop the art of reading good books? If you learn more about your Catholic heritage, your national heritage, and your cultural heritage, you'll have much more to discuss together.

What about our relationship?

Your own relationship is an important subject of communication, and it raises two questions. How do you communicate about the good things and how do you communicate about the irritations of life together?

Let me pass on an idea I picked up at a management seminar. Look for something that your spouse has done that day and compliment her or him for it. Every day. Husbands, you may have an easier time of this because generally the wives will be doing the meal preparation, and there will almost always be something you can find to compliment. On the other hand, if it's an unmitigated disaster, no need to fake it, but hold your tongue. She probably tried, and she's more disappointed than you are. A mutual sense of humor can be very helpful, but wait for her to make the first joke.

Wives, look for something, even if it's routine. Does your husband pick up his dirty clothes? Does he help you make the bed? Does he help with meals and the dishes? Does he take out the garbage? It's quite possible there are some husbands who don't, so be grateful for whom you have.

And if there's some disparity in this in favor of the wife receiving more compliments, so be it. The typical woman may be far more sensitive to this sort of thing than her husband, and if she's the primary "homemaker," she both deserves and needs an appreciative spouse.

How do we communicate about the irritations of married life?

Carefully. Very carefully. There's a fine line between nagging criticism and constructive communication, and the former is easier than the latter.

To avoid nagging, don't directly criticize the behavior of your spouse because that just sets the stage for a debate about the merits of that particular behavior. Instead, *describe your feelings* in reaction to a given behavior.

In the basic communication lessons given in the various 12-step recovery programs, people are taught to summarize their feelings into four basic categories. "When you do that, I feel GLAD or MAD or SAD or HURT."

The first point is this: no one can argue with you about your feelings. The merits of his going on a fishing trip every weekend or her going bowling several nights a week might be debated *ad nauseam,* but there can be no debate about the emotional reaction that such behavior may arouse in the spouse.

The second point is this: you may have to stop doing something which is not wrong in itself just because it is causing hurt or anger or sadness to your spouse. That's part of what marriage is about.

The third point should be obvious: don't fake your feelings to manipulate or to exercise control over your spouse.

The fourth point should also be obvious: no techniques can be an adequate substitute for love. Be sure to read and reread the "marriage recipes" of St. Paul in 1 Corinthians 13:1-7 and Ephesians 5:21-33.

The importance of civility.

I could not bring myself to form a question such as "Should we be civil to each other?" because the answer is so obvious.

Yet, civility can be overdone. Every once in a while you will read about some husband who deserts his wife who then tells everyone, "I didn't even know we had a problem." Certainly the husband had a problem, and just as obviously he didn't want to discuss it, but he remained civil toward her. Now if a man simply lets lust for another woman reign in his heart, he has some very big problems and may do everything possible to avoid giving any clues. He may be extremely civil and well mannered to his spouse—right up to desertion or filing for divorce.

However, apart from such deliberate deception, other spouses of good faith may fear that bringing up something which is really bothering her or him will disturb their pleasant civility, will rock the boat, and so they keep suppressing it, sometimes building up increasing resentment. Perhaps this is based on ungrounded fears or perhaps it is based on experience, and the latter raises another question.

Do I encourage open communication from my spouse?

If my spouse brings up something that is critical of me, no matter how indirectly and no matter how properly it is phrased in terms of feelings, do I react negatively? Do I immediately counter with my thoughts and feelings about something my spouse does or doesn't do? Do I blow up? Do I give my spouse the silent treatment for a few days? Do I hold a grudge? If I respond in an obviously negative way, am I not creating barriers to future communication?

Should we pray separately or together?

Both. If you want to live according to God's plan, if you want to receive the joys and blessings that God wants you to have, then doesn't it make sense that you will have to let Him into your marriage in a very realistic way? If you recognize that you need God's help to be the loving spouse and parent that both you and God want you to be, then pray daily for those graces.

I suggest that you start your day with the Morning Offering. If you are practicing systematic natural family planning, what better time for both husband and wife to pray silently than while the wife is taking her waking temperature for five minutes? (See chapter 9.) Grace before meals should be an every meal affair but yet not so routine you forget what you are doing. Mass every Sunday—together. Regular prayer before going to bed, and why not conclude your private prayer by praying together the Our Father, a Hail Mary, a Glory Be and an Act of Contrition? Are you planning to make love? Why not say a brief prayer together that your words and actions will help you to grow in true self-giving married love and that you will be good parents to any children whom God may give you?

You are bound by solemn obligation to worship at Mass every Sunday, but why settle for the minimum? If your schedule allows it, why not try to worship at least one extra day during the week? If you work in a downtown area, you may find a daily noontime Mass.

I strongly recommend that you both go to confession at least once a month. The Sacrament of Reconciliation (or Penance as it was called for centuries) has fallen into general disuse, but it is a powerful gift of the Lord. Regular monthly confession can really help you to grow in the Lord, and it is a powerful aid in overcoming temptations. Just the thought of confessing a sin to which you are tempted can be most helpful in overcoming the temptation.

When Our Lady appeared at Fatima in 1917, she asked that we pray the rosary every day for world peace, for the conversion of Russia, and for the conversion of sinners throughout the world. I pass on her request to you. It's a way of being part of the solution instead of being part of the problem.

On the other hand, if you live a life of practical atheism, even if you are a nominal Catholic, aren't you being part of the problem and don't you need to pray and to change? What's a life of practical atheism? Such a life gives no real place to God, and it is generally marked by contraception, perhaps occasional infidelity—certainly in thought and sometimes in deed. Other characteristics would include doing nothing to raise children in the ways of the Lord, no prayer life, no Sunday Mass every week, just the run of the mill completely secular married life that you see illustrated on television and in millions of lives in our post-Christian era. That many or even most such marriages end up in the divorce courts is hardly a surprise because the spouses in such marriages are simply not fulfilling God's plan for marriage.

What's the role of those three little words, "I love you"?

It's hard to imagine a spouse who doesn't like to hear those words, and yet the marriage books typically have a story about a marriage in which those words are never spoken. The classic example is the faithful husband who works hard to provide for his wife and children and thinks that his actions are proof enough of his love. Well, gentlemen, it's true that actions speak louder than words, but wives still like to hear the words. And wives, husbands like to hear them too.

It's very easy to say them while making love, almost too easy, so a suggestion: conclude your evening prayers to God with that important statement to each other, "I love you."

What are some typical examples of non-verbal communication?

Body language is another term for non-verbal communication, and it covers a wide range of possible actions from holding hands to deliberately avoiding your spouse.

Personal appearance is a form of body language. The way you dress and the way you keep yourself up can say to your spouse, "You're important to me." I'm hardly suggesting dress-up clothes around the house, but it can mean something to a husband to come home to a wife who looks neat and feminine rather than her grubbiest, (and my personal opinion is that a wife looks far more feminine in a denim skirt than in jeans). Likewise, it can mean something to a wife to have her husband come to the table neat and clean rather than looking his grubbiest.

The kind of greeting you give when your spouse returns home from work can be a non-verbal form of communication. There's a big difference between "Oh, you're home" and a brief hug and a kiss.

A smile is a good communicator. For some people, a smile comes very easy; others have to work at it, especially after years of hard work and problems. Still, it's something worth working at.

Ordinary good manners show respect for those around you; they need not be reserved just for company.

As mentioned above, the tone and volume of your voice and your facial expressions are body language expressions which mix in an inseparable way with the words you say.

What about sex as communication?

Sexual intercourse is a unique form of communication; it is reserved exclusively to those who are married to each other. It is intended by God to be at least implicitly a renewal of your marriage covenant. One of the challenges of marriage is to make this renewal more explicit in your own hearts and minds.

Part of that challenge is this: to move from a concentration or concern for the satisfaction of your own sexual desires to the pleasing of your spouse. And it works both ways—from having relations when you don't particularly feel like it to making an effort to make it a pleasing experience for your spouse. And sometimes it means not requesting relations when you know that your spouse would much prefer either sleep or some other form of communication.

Please, never forget that sexual communication is of special concern to the Lord. It is the subject of 20% of the Ten Commandments (actually 29% of the seven Commandments concerning other people). God is Love, and sexual intercourse is widely—and correctly—regarded as a special expression of love. So God is very concerned that what is *called* an act of love by man and woman who are made in his image and likeness be in reality a *true* act of love. That's the basis for the Church's concern about methods of birth control as described in the next chapter.

What is the effect of television on marital communication?

In a word, it can be deadly. Have you ever heard of anyone saying that watching commercial, secular television is good for their marriage or for any marriage?

First of all, if you sit by yourself in front of a TV screen to watch a canned show, it may be a statement that you prefer such fare to active communication. At the least, it can intrude seriously on your "couple time."

Second, what you see is generally unreal. The news is highly edited to reflect what the producers want you to see, and the so-called family shows, not just the sex and violence productions, are unreal. Man by nature is religious, but you will not find that reflected in most movies and TV shows. The wives/mothers are generally not just ordinarily attractive but almost always extremely attractive. The husbands/fathers typically are either buffoons or are so wise and unflappable that ordinary husbands/dads can't possibly compete.

Third, much of what you see is the source of real temptation to the average man. The ads with their super-sexy women in blatantly suggestive situations are intended to create a fantasy, and they are effective. The ordinary man has enough sexual stimulation from his own wife and his own hormones. He does not need the TV fantasies to give him additional ideas.

He does not need to be made to feel sorry for himself that his wife is not like the glamorous, aggressive sex kittens constantly portrayed in the ads for beer, bras, perfumes, shaving aids, etc.

This is not to say that there are not some fine television shows; it is possible for a couple to watch some TV fare as genuine passive recreation and to enjoy each other's company while doing so. However, even the best of shows can be ruined by the ads.

A special note needs to be made about watching sports. It can be very time consuming. I think the wife who feels hurt because her husband is spending most of Sunday glued to the TV set, oblivious to spouse and children, has a legitimate subject for communication, negotiation, and reduction. It's one thing to watch one game; it's something else to watch two or three, and the ads are sometimes among the worst.

For discussion with your fiance:

Although these questions are written from the perspective of a married couple, project into the future and answer them as best you can. Then compare your answers with those of your fiance.

(O − Often; S = Sometimes; N = Never)

	O	S	N
Do I compliment my spouse?	___	___	___
Do I nag?	___	___	___
Do I manipulate my spouse's feelings?	___	___	___
Am I sarcastic?	___	___	___
Do I suppress things that bother me and let them build up?	___	___	___
Do I share my feelings about things that bother me?	___	___	___
If so, do I share them in a civil manner?	___	___	___
If and when criticized . . .			
Do I counter with something negative about my spouse?	___	___	___
Do I blow up?	___	___	___
Do I respond with the "silent treatment"?	___	___	___
Do I hold a grudge?	___	___	___

Do I pray by myself?   _____ _____ _____
Do I pray aloud with my spouse?   _____ _____ _____
Do we worship together at Mass?   _____ _____ _____
Do I say, "I love you"?   _____ _____ _____
Do I say "goodbye" with a hug or a kiss?   _____ _____ _____
Do I turn off the TV to spend time with
my spouse?   _____ _____ _____
Do I make judgments before hearing
all the facts?   _____ _____ _____
Am I easily distracted when my
spouse talks to me?   _____ _____ _____
Am I often too pre-occupied to be a
good listener?   _____ _____ _____
Do I think my feelings are more impor-
tant than my spouse's?   _____ _____ _____

8. Birth Control

Catholic teaching about birth control is very clear; it is also very much misunderstood in two different ways. Sometimes the plain facts are not known; at other times the bare facts are known but only superficially. As with much else about Christian marriage, Catholic teaching on birth control can be truly understood only in the light of Christian discipleship.

Why did Jesus become one of us?

Catholics believe that Jesus came to save us and to teach us the truth about love— God's love for each one of us and how we are to love each other. That means that He teaches us the divine truth about human love. It also means that our pursuit of love and happiness must always be in the light of first responding to the Lord: "Whoever would save his life will lose it; and whoever loses his life for my sake, he will save it." (Lk 9:24).

Note well that Jesus promises not only eternal happiness in heaven to those who follow Him on the narrow way (Mt 7:14); He also promises a special peace and joy here and now on earth to those who really accept Him and his way. "Come to me, all who labor and are heavy laden, and I will give you rest. Take my yoke upon you, and learn from Me; for I am gentle and lowly in heart, and you will find rest for your souls. For my yoke is easy and my burden is light" (Mt 11: 28-30).

If Catholic teaching about birth control is so clear, why does there seem to be a lot of confusion about it?

To illustrate that the teaching is clear, this chapter will quote many documents of the Church. As to why there seems to be confusion, who can say for sure? Some people—even priests, educators, and marriage ministers—appear to be simply ignorant about the well-documented teaching; I suspect that others find it difficult to transmit a teaching that may involve the daily cross for many, and so they try to interpret it away or say other things that confuse couples seeking guidance.

What does the Catholic Church teach about having children?

For centuries, the Church has taught that in a very real sense the primary purpose of marriage (and marital relations) is having children and raising them in the ways of the Lord; the secondary purpose is to build up the marriage relationship. Look at it this way: the only natural and moral way to co-create a new person destined for eternal life with God is through marital relations; there are, however, many ways in which you can build your marriage relationship. Note well that *both* of these purposes are part of loving one's spouse truly.

For pastoral reasons, the Fathers of Vatican Council II (1962-1965) did not use the traditional "primary and secondary" terminology, but there is no doubt that they reaffirmed the traditional teaching in what follows:

> Marriage and conjugal love are by their nature ordained toward the begetting and educating of children. Children are really the supreme gift of marriage and contribute very substantially to the welfare of their parents. The God Himself who said, "It is not good for man to be alone" (Gn 2:18) and "who made man from the beginning male and female" (Mt 19:4), wished to share with man a certain special participation in his own creative work. Thus He blessed male and female, saying: "Increase and multiply" (Gn 1:28).
>
> Hence, while not making the other purposes of matrimony of less account, the true practice of conjugal love, and the whole meaning of the family life which results from it, have this aim: that the couple be ready with stout hearts to cooperate with the love of the Creator and the Savior, Who through them will enlarge and enrich his own family day by day.
>
> Parents should regard as their proper mission the task of transmitting human life and educating those to whom it has been transmitted. They should realize that they are thereby cooperators with the love of God the Creator, and are, so to speak, the interpreters of that love" (*Gaudium et Spes, n. 50*).*

Does the Church teach that a couple must have as many children as they physically can?

No. The Church clearly teaches that if you have a sufficiently serious

---

* Vatican Council II, *Pastoral Constitution on the Church in the Modern World,* 17 December 1965. Subsequent references are solely within the text and use the common Latin name of this document, *Gaudium et Spes.* References are to numbered sections in the official text.

reason for avoiding pregnancy, you may use the natural methods of family planning.

> If, then, there are serious motives to space out births, which derive from the physical or psychological conditions of husband and wife, or from external conditions, the Church teaches that it is then licit to take into account the natural rhythms immanent in the generative functions, for the use of marriage in the infecund periods [infertile times] only, and in this way to regulate birth without offending the moral principles which have been recalled earlier (*Humanae Vitae,* 16).[1]

What are serious reasons for avoiding pregnancy?

For many couples, the hardest thing about the practice of natural family planning is precisely this question: Do we have a sufficiently serious reason to be avoiding pregnancy? Why aren't we inviting the Lord to bless us with a child or another child? Should we?

The Church does not provide us with hard and fast rules in the area of family size. Rather, in decisions about family size, the married couple

> will thoughtfully take into account both their own welfare and that of their children, those already born and those which may be foreseen. For this accounting they will reckon with both the material and the spiritual conditions of the times as well as of their state in life. Finally, they will consult the interests of the family group, of temporal society, and of the Church itself (*Gaudium et Spes,* 50).

That's very broad, and it has to be taken in the context of the previous statement from the same document quoted above. Approximately three years after Vatican II, Pope Paul VI issued *Humanae Vitae* which noted the need for "serious reasons" (*H.V.,*10), "just reasons," "worthy and weighty reasons," and again "just reasons" for delaying pregnancy or limiting family size (all in *H.V.,* 16).

Isn't there a population problem and doesn't that justify birth control?

The population problem of the West is a birth rate which for years has been below replacement level; Ireland has been the only exception. In Europe this native depopulation has led to planned immigration to keep the factories running.

To the extent that large or growing populations might be a problem in some parts of the world, that would be the "interests of . . . temporal society" and the "external conditions" mentioned above by Vatican II and *Humanae Vitae*, that is, reasons to justify the use of natural family planning.

The "population bomb" enthusiasts of the late Sixties and their gloomy predictions have been thoroughly discredited by subsequent events, but they still have a near monopoly hold on the popular media. For a balanced view, you will have to look elsewhere as indicated in the references at the end of this chapter.[2]

Why is the Catholic Church opposed to unnatural forms of birth control?

The basic reason for the Church's opposition to any sort of sinful action is that such actions are contrary to the nature God has given us.

The meaning and purposes of sexual intercourse stem from the nature of marriage and our own created human nature. Sexual intercourse is intended by God to be exclusively a marriage act, and what Jesus said about marriage applies also to the marriage act: "What therefore God has joined together, let not man put asunder" (Mk 10:9). To paraphrase, "When God has joined marital relations and fertility, let no one take it apart."

Think about that for a moment. Who put together in one action both what we call "making love" and "making babies"? Who else but God? The essence of the contraceptive mentality is this: "We can take apart what God has put together." The Church keeps reminding us that we have no moral right to do so.

Note also what has happened in the American contraceptive culture. First, in the 1920s and 1930s there was a growing social acceptance of contraception, first among the irreligious and then among Protestants. (Catholics generally followed the teaching of the Church until the late Sixties and then hopped on the contraception bandwagon with a vengeance.) Then, growing acceptance of taking apart what God has joined together led to increased social acceptance of divorce and remarriage. That was followed by a denial that God has put together marriage and sex, i.e., that sexual intercourse is intended by God to be exclusively a marriage act, and we witnessed the acting out of the sexual revolution from the Sixties to the present time. Next, having divorced procreation from marital relations and sex from marriage, Western culture in the Eighties and Nineties has increasingly accepted homosexual sodomy as just another lifestyle, for Western culture has lost the basis on which to judge the objective morality

72

of sexual actions. After all, the sodomist might argue, the whole purpose of marital contraception is to make marital relations just as sterile as the sexual acts of homosexuals.

Lastly, consider the tremendous amount of human pain and suffering caused by the sexual revolution which essentially started with the acceptance of marital contraception. Practically every week you can read some new report which chronicles the disastrous effects of the sexual revolution, whether it be the growing recognition of the psychological harm done to children by divorce or desertion, or the spread of AIDS, or increased infertility, or abortion.

It is so obvious that anyone can see it: the Commandments are for our benefit, not God's. The Catholic Church must oppose unnatural forms of birth control because it is the solemn duty of the Church to proclaim the Commandments as part of God's love for us.

Is there an ideal family size?

The Church has no specific teaching about an ideal family size. As indicated above, couples may take many factors into consideration. On the other hand, there is a general Christian warning against decision making based solely on materialistic factors. Life is a gift to be shared, and the Christian couple are called to be generous in the service of life according to their circumstances.

For example, Pope John Paul II has noted that

> decisions about the number of children and the sacrifices
> to be made for them must not be taken only with a view to
> adding comfort and preserving a peaceful existence.
> Reflecting upon this matter before God, with the graces
> drawn from the Sacrament, and guided by the teaching of
> the Church, parents will remind themselves that it is
> certainly less serious to deny their children certain com-
> forts or material advantages than to deprive them of the
> presence of brothers or sisters who could help them to
> grow in humanity and to realize the beauty of life at all
> ages and in all its variety (Washington Mall, 1979).[3]

In short, marriage is about family, not mutual egoism. Life is a great gift to be shared generously, for your children are called to live with God — and with you and your spouse — for all eternity. Since there is absolutely nothing in the Gospel of Jesus to indicate that feeling comfortable is a criterion for moral judgment, it is fairly safe to say that except in rare circumstances, you are probably called to have children beyond the easy comfort level. The best advice would be not to set any size — whether two or ten children — in your early years of marriage. Rather, determine to be open to the Lord's calling, and make your decisions as you move through your married life together. If you are consciously raising your children in the ways of the Lord, you will find many more joys in your family than are found by your secularized neighbors.

What does the Church teach about methods of birth control?

The Fathers of Vatican II taught the principles that must be used:
When there is a question of harmonizing conjugal love with the responsible transmission of life, the moral aspect of any procedure does not depend solely on sincere intentions or on an evaluation of motives. It must be determined by objective standards. These, based on the nature of the human person and his acts, preserve the full sense of mutual self-giving and human procreation in the context of true love. Such a goal cannot be achieved unless the virtue of conjugal chastity is sincerely practiced.

Relying on these principles, sons of the Church may not undertake methods of regulating procreation which are found blameworthy by the teaching authority of the Church in its unfolding of the divine law (*Gaudium et Spes,* 51).

Does the Church teach that unnatural or artificial means of birth control are immoral and blameworthy?

Yes. In *Humanae Vitae*, abortion is the first-named immoral form of birth control (n.14).

The teaching then condemns tubal ligations, vasectomies, and the Pill:
Equally to be excluded, as the teaching authority of the Church has frequently declared, is direct sterilization, whether perpetual or temporary, whether of the man or woman (*H.V.,* n.14).

The text continues with wording that condemns as immoral all other unnatural forms of birth control. This includes the Pill, the intrauterine device (IUD), foams, diaphragms, condoms, withdrawal, mutual and solitary masturbation, and sodomitic practices:

> Similarly excluded is every action which, either in antici-
> pation of the conjugal act, or in its accomplishment, or in
> the development of its natural consequences, proposes,
> whether as an end or as a means, to render procreation
> impossible (*H.V.*, n.14).

Are some forms of unnatural birth control worse than others?

Yes. Those forms that act after conception has occurred to prevent the continuation of the pregnancy participate in the additional evil of abortion.

> From the moment of its conception life must be guarded
> with greatest care, while abortion and infanticide are
> unspeakable crimes (*Gaudium et Spes,* 51).

Surgical abortion is the most obvious but not the only form of abortion. The IUD has the potential to act as an early abortion agent by preventing implantation of the week-old human life.

The birth control Pill and implants such as Norplant make the inner lining of the uterus very hostile to implantation. It is not known precisely how often the Pill or implant acts as an abortifacient (abortion-causing agent), but it cannot be denied that the Pill or implant may be causing an early abortion in any given cycle in any given woman. A birth control researcher found solid evidence that a low dosage combination Pill allowed ovulation to occur in 4.7% of cycles. If standard conception probability rates (.25 per cycle) are applied to that ovulation rate, the 13.8 million American women on the Pill (in 1988) would be inducing 2.1 million very early abortions each year, even more than the number of bloody surgical abortions.[4]

What about Natural Family Planning?

As noted above, the Church explicitly teaches that it is morally permissible to practice natural family planning if you have sufficiently serious reasons to avoid pregnancy. With that qualification, the Church is warning against selfishness in limiting the size of your family.

Should we learn Natural Family Planning?

Definitely yes, regardless of your current thinking about family size. Pope John Paul II teaches that through an informed awareness of their fertility,

God the Creator invites the spouses not to be passive operators but rather "cooperators or almost interpreters" of his plan (*Gaudium et Spes,* n.50). In fact they are called, out of respect for the objective moral order established by God, to an obligatory discernment of the indications of God's will concerning their family. Thus in relationship to physical, psychological and social conditions, responsible parenthood will be able to be expressed "either by the deliberate and generous decision to raise a large family, or by the decision, made for serious moral reasons and with due respect for the moral law, to avoid for the time being, or even for an indeterminate period, another birth" (*H.V.,* n.10).[5]

In short, spouses are obliged to try to discern God's will for them regarding their family. Are they not also obliged to learn their mutual fertility so they can carry out God's will? Even if they decide to have a large family, they should still learn their fertility; they need to know when to abstain if the wife is taking medication that might harm a baby in her womb, etc. They also need to learn how to do the "ecological" breastfeeding that will ordinarily space babies about two years apart—God's original and still excellent plan for spacing babies. (More about this in the next chapter.)

Since both the natural and the unnatural methods of birth control have the purpose of limiting family size, aren't they morally the same?

Not at all. The end does not justify the means; a common purpose does not make morally equal all the possible means of achieving that purpose. "It is not licit, even for the gravest reasons, to do evil so that good may follow therefrom" (*H.V.,* 14).

A prime purpose of the Ten Commandments is to teach us that we may not act against our created human nature in pursuing some purpose or pleasure. Thus, we may not kill or steal or commit adultery—or contracept—to advance ourselves. The Church teaches that efforts at birth regulation "must be done with respect for the order established by God" (*H.V.,* 16).

You can see this point very easily by using a different example. A couple may want to live in a nice house that they cannot easily pay for. Would that desire justify his making money in the immoral drug trade or her earning money as a prostitute? Of course not. Everyone with any sense of morality recognizes you can't do those evils in order to get your dream house faster than by frugally saving the results of hard and honest work. Everyone with any sense of morality recognizes that the moral principle, "The end does not justify the means," applies here. It applies also to the various methods of birth control.

How is contraception viewed in terms of the marriage covenant?

In the marriage act—that is, normal, completed marital sexual intercourse—the bodily union of the spouses symbolizes the unity-from-gift-of-self they created when they first married. However, in every form of contraceptive birth control, there is a positive effort to hold back that gift of self. That contradicts the nature of the marriage covenant, and such going against their marriage covenant helps to explain why couples who use unnatural forms of birth control have such a high divorce rate.

Consider your marriage covenant; consider how you will promise your caring love and fidelity, for better and for worse "until death do us part." Then consider that God intends that sexual intercourse should be at least implicitly an affirmation, a renewal, of your marriage covenant. Lastly, consider what the body language of contraception says: "I take you for better but *not* for the imagined worse of possible pregnancy."

What would be the status of your marriage if you said at the time of your wedding, "I take you for better but *not* for worse"? It simply would not be a marriage. It would be called an invalid marriage; it would be dishonest and therefore immoral to engage in "marital relations" because you wouldn't be married. By the same token, unnatural forms of birth control render marital relations invalid as a renewal of your marriage covenant. In short, contraceptive marital intercourse is dishonest; it pretends to be a true marriage act when it is not. It is not true to the very nature of marriage, and that is probably the most basic reason why the Church teaches—and will continue to teach—that it is immoral for married couples to use unnatural forms of birth control.

Is there a biblical basis for the Church's teaching against contraception?

Yes; the 38th Chapter of Genesis tells the story of Judah, his sons, and Tamar. One of the sons, Onan, practiced the sin of contraception—withdrawal in this case—with Tamar, and the Bible tells us that God killed him because he had done an abominable thing (Gn 38:10).

It is recognized today that Judah, Onan and a younger brother were all guilty of violating an ancient Eastern brotherhood custom called the "Law of the Levirate" (Deut 25:5-6). (If a man died without leaving a son, his brother had to take the widow as a wife, and their first son would be considered to be the son of the dead brother in order to keep his name alive.) However, the punishment for violating that law was very mild and is spelled out in Deuteronomy 25:7-10. Judah himself admitted his guilt (Gn 38:26). It is therefore clear that the special punishment meted out to Onan was not just for the violation of the Levirate but rather for the way in which only he had sinned—his contraceptive behavior of going through the motions of the covenantal act and then "spilling his seed" (Gn 38:9).

This interpretation is reinforced by the only incident in the New Testament where immediate death is the punishment for sin—the deaths of Ananias and Saphira who went through the motions of a giving act but defrauded it of its meaning (Acts 5:1-11).

Are there any other biblical references to birth control?

Probably yes. In the New Testament, the Greek "pharmakeia" probably refers to birth control. "Pharmakeia" in general was the mixing of potions for secret purposes, and it is known that potions were mixed in the first century A.D. to prevent or stop a pregnancy—just as with the Pill today. The typical translation as "sorcery" does not reveal all of the specific practices condemned by the New Testament. In all four of the passages in which it appears, it is in a context condemning sexual immorality (Gal 5:19-26; Rev 9:21, 21:8, 22:15; three of the four passages also condemn murder). Thus it is probable that there are four New Testament passages condemning the use of the products of "pharmakeia" for birth control purposes. The eminent scholar, Fr. John A. Hardon, S.J., puts it this way:

> Given the widespread contraceptive practice of the first century of the Christian era, euphemistically referred to as "using magic" and "using drugs," it is logical to see in the New Testament prohibition of *mageia* and *pharmakeia* an implicit condemnation of contraception. This is especially true when the contexts refer to sins against chastity.[6]

Does the Bible have anything to say about human love and sexuality?

By all means, yes. There is simply no doubt that the entire biblical notion of human love points to the fact that men and woman are called to subordinate "eros," romantic or erotic love, to "agape" (ah-gah-pay), self-giving love. While not referring specifically to the issue of birth control, St. Paul's most famous discourse on love is still applicable to this discussion. It is noteworthy that he begins and ends on the two aspects of love that are so needed for marriage and also for the happy practice of natural family planning. "Love is always patient and kind; ... it is always ready ... to endure whatever comes" (1Cor 13:4, 7, Jerusalem Bible translation). Christian husbands are also told to love their wives as Christ loved the Church and sacrificed Himself for her (Eph 5:25). All Christians were told by Christ on the night before his death to love one another as He loves us, a statement that has obvious overtones about self-giving love (Jn 15:12). St. Paul also tells his listeners that the fruits of the Spirit are "love, joy, peace, patience, kindness, goodness, faithfulness, gentleness, self-control." He reminds us that we cannot really belong to Christ unless we "have crucified the flesh with its passions and desires" (Gal 5:22-24).

The above is incomplete but it serves one limited purpose. It shows that it is perfectly legitimate to state that the religious doctrine of marital non-contraception has a basis in Scripture and that the practice of natural family planning with its necessity of a certain amount of sexual self-control fits well within the Christian biblical tradition.

Wouldn't it be helpful if the Bible contained condemnations of contraception that were more explicit and more frequent?

Not really. The lack of multiple references doesn't disturb the person who has a sense of realism about what God is saying to us in Christ and also understands what's happening today. Such a person is aware that the Bible could hardly be more explicit in its condemnation of homosexual sodomy (e.g. Romans 1:26-32), but he or she knows that those who want to try to justify sodomy simply dismiss the biblical texts as not relevant to today, or they interpret St. Paul to mean "promiscuous" sodomy although the Apostle makes no such distinctions. Even if the Bible were filled with explicit condemnations of abortion, sterilization, and contraception, the same approach would be used on such texts by those who wished to try to justify such behaviors as compatible with biblical Christianity.

The dismissal of bothersome texts or their interpretation into nothingness helps to explain Roman Catholic belief that Jesus did not leave us with only a book subject to everyone's personal and sometimes contradictory interpretations but also established his Church as an authoritative teacher guided by the Holy Spirit. The constant teaching by the Church on a matter of faith and morals is called Tradition.

The earliest non-biblical Christian writing is called the *Didache* ("The

Teaching of the Twelve Apostles"); it dates back to the first century. Father Hardon notes:

> The *Didache*, which explicitly condemned abortion, also implicitly condemned contraception. The early Christians were told in four successive precepts: "You shall not use magic. You shall not use drugs. You shall not procure abortion. You shall not destroy a newborn child (II, 2).[7]

Is the Christian doctrine against unnatural birth control a new teaching?

No. The question of birth control has been raised many times for 20 centuries of Christian life, and the Church has always responded with a firm and universal negative to abortion, sterilization and all unnatural forms of birth control. Until recently, the word used for all forms of contraceptive behaviors was simply "onanism" from the sin of Onan. The encyclical *Humanae Vitae* in 1968 simply reaffirmed this universal Tradition.

Does this constant teaching have any special significance?

Yes. At the Last Supper, Jesus promised repeatedly that the Holy Spirit would lead his Church into the fullness of the truth (John, chapters 14-17). When a teaching has been taught with such unanimity and constancy throughout the centuries, those who believe in Christ have every reason to believe that such a teaching is from the Holy Spirit and therefore true. Some theologians are convinced that the constancy of this teaching fulfills all the requirements set forth by Vatican II for its being taught infallibly by the universal ordinary magisterium of the Church.[8]

Have Protestant churches shared in this Tradition?

Yes. Martin Luther called onanism a form of sodomy, John Calvin called it a form of homicide, and John Wesley said that those who practice unnatural forms of birth control would lose their souls.[9] The strength of Protestant conviction is reflected in the fact that the American anti-contraception laws of the 1870s were passed by essentially Protestant legislatures for a basically Protestant United States.

Before 1930, no Protestant church accepted contraception, sterilization or abortion. On August 14, 1930, the Church of England broke away from the previously unanimous teaching and became the first church to accept what it called unnatural forms of birth control; and most, but not all, Protestant churches have unfortunately followed that path. To repeat, before

1930, the immorality of contraception was taught by Catholics and Protestants alike; it was not an issue of disagreement.

Have churches that accepted contraception also accepted abortion?

Tragically, yes. Many of the church bodies that accepted contraception also have come to call killing unborn babies something that a Christian may do.

Do non-Christian religions have similar teachings on birth control?

It is difficult to find specific moral teachings in some of the non-Christian world religions. However, there is no doubt that the most famous Hindu of modern times, Mahatma Gandhi, was completely opposed to unnatural birth control. He called for self-control, and his statements in the 1920s have many similarities to the statements of *Humanae Vitae* in 1968.

What is the significance of priests or theologians who appear confused or not to believe the official teaching of the Church?

The chief significance is that people need to distinguish between the authentic teaching of the Church and that of some theologians. In 1973 the Canadian bishops responded to this question with a *Statement on the Formation of Conscience.*

> "To follow one's conscience" and to remain a Catholic, one must take into account first and foremost the teaching of the magisterium. When doubt arises due to a conflict of "my" views and those of the magisterium, the presumption of truth lies on the part of the magisterium. [The *magisterium* is the official teaching authority of the Church—the Pope and the bishops in union with him.] . . . And this must be carefully distinguished from the teaching of individual theologians or individual priests, however intelligent or persuasive.[10]

Has there ever been such confusion before?

Yes. This is not the place for a history of such things, but special mention might be made of the problems of the 16th and 17th centuries when theologians went wild with moral heresies in both directions, laxism and rigorism.

81

Has the teaching of *Humanae Vitae* been backed up by bishops throughout the world?

Yes. With the exception of a very small number of hierarchies, every national body of bishops which has commented on *Humanae Vitae* has supported it. Even where positive support was not offered, there was no real divergence from the teaching of the encyclical.

In the United States, the Catholic bishops reaffirmed the Tradition immediately after *Humanae Vitae*,[11] again in their specifically moral pastoral document,[12] and again in a major document on religious education.[13]

What about Pope John Paul II?

Pope John Paul II made this teaching about the truth of love the central point of his teaching efforts in the first ten years of his pontificate (1978-1988). His manner of speaking and the frequency of his affirmations leave no doubt that this teaching fulfills all the criteria of Vatican II for a teaching that must be accepted by all believing Catholics.[14]

Summary.

Jesus sacrificed his life that we might share eternal life with Him, and throughout the Gospel, Jesus teaches us that love is not always easy. He teaches that in married love man and wife are called to love each other until death. He shocked his listeners by teaching that divorce and remarriage constitute adultery, as we have seen in Chapter 4. At the Last Supper He gave us the new commandment, one that most of us find quite difficult: "Love one another even as I have loved you" (Jn 13:35). But all of this is the divine truth about human love.

The Catholic Church continues to teach that it is seriously immoral to use unnatural methods of birth control, to defraud the meaning of the marriage act by seeking to take apart what God has put together. This, too, is part of the divine truth about human love.

Answer and discuss with your fiance:

1. T   F   Vatican Council II reaffirmed that marriage by
                   its nature is for the procreation and education of
                   children.

2. T   F   The Church teaches that a couple must have a sufficiently serious reason to avoid pregnancy to justify the use of natural family planning.

3. T   F   The Church teaches that it is immoral, i.e., sinful, to use sterilization and other unnatural forms of birth control for any reason.

4. T   F   The birth control pill sometimes acts as an early abortion agent.

5. T   F   Natural Family Planning differs from unnatural methods of birth control since it does not act against the created nature God has given us.

6. T   F   The use of unnatural forms of birth control makes the marital embrace say, "I take you for better but definitely not for the imagined worse of possible pregnancy" and thus contradicts the marital meaning of sex.

7. T   F   Christian teaching against unnatural forms of birth control has been consistent for twenty centuries.

8. T   F   Before 1930, no Christian Church had formally accepted contraception as morally acceptable.

References

1. Pope Paul VI, encyclical letter titled *Humanae Vitae* ("On Human Life") 25 July 1968. References are to numbered sections within the official text.

2. Jacqueline Kasun, *The War Against Population: The Economics and Ideology of World Population Control* (San Francisco: Ignatius Press, 1988) 225 pp. Also: *Population Research Institute Review*, a bi-monthly newsletter published by the Population Research Institute, P.O. Box 2024, Baltimore MD 21298-9559, USA. Also: J. Richard Neuhaus, *In Defense of People* (New York: Macmillan, 1971).

3. John Paul II, homily at Mass on the Washington Mall, 7 October 1979.

4. Paul Weckenbrock, R.Ph., *The Pill: Is It Safe? How Does It Work?* (Cincinnati: Couple to Couple League, 1993).

5. "Pope calls spouses to a sense of responsibility for love and life," *L'Osservatore Romano*, weekly English edition, 17 December 1990, 1-3.

6. John A. Hardon, S.J., *The Catholic Catechism* (New York: Doubleday, 1975) p. 367.

7. John A. Hardon, S.J., p. 367.

8. For various arguments about the infallibility of the teaching of *Humanae Vitae,* see John F. Kippley, *Sex and the Marriage Covenant: A Basis for Morality* (Cincinnati: Couple to Couple League, 1991) 148-169.

9. Charles D. Provan, *The Bible and Birth Control* (Monongahela, PA 15063: Zimmer Printing, 1989) 81, 68, 91.

10. Canadian Catholic Conference, *Statement on the Formation of Conscience,* n. 41, 12 December 1973.

11. National Council of Catholic Bishops, *Human Life in Our Day,* 15 November 1968.

12. NCCB, *To Live in Christ Jesus*, 11 November 1976, nn. 45-49.

13. NCCB, *Sharing the Light of Faith*, 1979, nn. 105b, 131.

14. For an extensive reivew of the teaching of Pope John Paul II on birth control, see J. Kippley, *Sex and the Marriage Covenant*, chapter 6.

All answers to the quiz are true.

9. Natural Family Planning

In his Providence, God has provided natural means of birth regulation which are sufficient for our needs. From the creation of the first family, breastfeeding has provided a certain amount of spacing between babies. More recently, other, more systematic natural methods have been developed.

What is Natural Family Planning?

Natural Family Planning (NFP) generally refers to the practice of achieving or avoiding pregnancy through an informed awareness of the wife's fertile and infertile times. It also refers to the spacing of babies through the form of nursing called "ecological breastfeeding."

What is the scientific basis of systematic NFP?

It is well established that during each menstrual cycle a woman normally becomes fertile and then naturally infertile. The fertile time is the part of her cycle when sexual intercourse can result in pregnancy. A woman's body provides certain physical signs which indicate her fertile and infertile times.

You learned in your grade school or high school science courses that the essence of the scientific method is the systematic observation and recording of recurring events. That's precisely what makes NFP the only scientific method of family planning. The wife briefly observes and records her signs of fertility and infertility each day.

What are the signs of fertility and infertility?

The most used signs are a normal discharge of cervical mucus and changes in a woman's waking temperature. Other signs include physical changes in her cervix and a feeling in the area of her ovaries called "ovulation pain."

Cervical mucus is nature's way of helping a man's sperm reach a woman's egg. Her flow of cervical mucus generally starts in a small way several days before she ovulates (releases an egg); it is a very positive sign that her fertile time has started. About the time she ovulates, her cervical mucus may be abundant and have a consistency something like raw egg-white. After ovulation, her mucus normally disappears.

A woman's waking temperature is lower before ovulation and rises slightly but distinctly after ovulation. After it has been well elevated for several days (while her mucus has been disappearing), it is a very positive sign that she is infertile.

What is the Sympto-Thermal Method of Natural Family Planning?

The Sympto-Thermal Method is a system of using the mucus and temperature signs in a crosschecking way for the highest confidence and reliability in family planning. The other signs (changes in the cervix and "ovulation pain") are also used by many women.

What is the Ovulation Method of Natural Family Planning?

The Ovulation Method is a system which uses only the mucus sign. It also uses only one way of observing the cervical mucus. Though not providing the crosscheck of another sign, it works well for many women, and it is the preferred method in those parts of the world in which it is impossible or very difficult to obtain thermometers.

What is the Rhythm Method?

The Rhythm Method is the Calendar Rhythm Method developed in 1930. It was based on the scientific discoveries in the 1920s about the time relationship between ovulation and the next menstruation, but it was based only on general averages and past cycle history, not current history. Therefore it was not a scientific method based on current observations as are the modern methods — the Sympto-Thermal Method and the Ovulation Method. It was the 1930's model of NFP, and great progress has been made since then.

Does NFP work with irregular cycles?

Yes. Modern NFP assumes that every woman has irregular cycles at least some of the time. In general, if her fertile time comes earlier or later than usual, she knows about it because the start of her cervical mucus comes earlier or later.

Does NFP take much time?

No. With NFP's Sympto-Thermal Method, a woman needs just a few minutes to take her temperature when she wakes each morning. What better time for her morning prayers? During the day she takes a moment now and then to become aware of her cervical mucus. Her husband records a dot for her temperature on a chart, and at night she records a symbol to describe the absence or presence of any cervical mucus. This simple process gives them an accurate, day-to-day picture of her fertility.

NFP: Safe, Healthy, and Effective. What does that mean?

Safe: Natural Family Planning uses no birth control devices or drugs. Every drug has potential side effects and should be taken only when necessary to cure or relieve an illness, etc. But fertility is a normal process, not a disease. Birth control pills and implants are unnecessary drugs, and most intrauterine devices (IUDs) were taken off the American market because of health-related lawsuits. In addition, some physicians have linked spermicides with birth defects.

Healthy: NFP is health enhancing. Through NFP charting, a woman becomes aware of her normal fertility-menstrual cycle. Some kinds of cycle irregularities can alert her to possible underlying problems, and she can seek early health-care assistance.

Effective: Numerous studies, including one by the U.S. government, have shown that the Sympto-Thermal Method of NFP can be used at the 99% level of effectiveness for avoiding pregnancy.[1] That's equal to the birth control pill and better than any of the barrier methods.

Can NFP help to *achieve* pregnancy?

Yes. This question may seem irrelevant to you as an engaged couple because most engaged and newly married couples consider themselves highly fertile and imagine that they will be able to become pregnant whenever they want to. That's not necessarily so. The number of infertile couples has increased in the Pill Era; some couples are almost absolutely infertile; others are only marginally fertile. NFP helps you to achieve pregnancy in three ways.

1. The absence of chemicals and devices does nothing to harm your fertility.

2. With NFP you will become aware of the most fertile days in your overall fertile time, and you will learn how to maximize your mutual fertility.

3. If you are of marginal fertility, your charted cycles may reveal certain patterns that can contribute to infertility and which can sometimes be corrected simply by better nutrition. Many couples of marginal fertility are helped by NFP training to achieve much wanted pregnancies, and the charts of those who may need medical help can assist the knowledgeable physician.

Does breastfeeding space babies?

Yes. More pregnancies are postponed throughout the world through breastfeeding than by any of the methods that can be called conscious efforts at birth regulation. However, this is true only when a mother practices a very natural form of baby care characterized by mother-baby closeness. This is called "ecological breastfeeding" to distinguish it from "cultural breastfeeding" which does not space babies.

The usual spacing of babies with ecological breastfeeding ranges between 18 and 30 months; the average is about 24 months. It certainly seems that the Author of Nature has designed Nature so that mothers should be with their babies, enjoy a close nursing relationship, and also enjoy a natural spacing of babies.[2]

Is Natural Family Planning "natural"?

In other words, is it natural for a married couple to practice sexual self-control? Yes. No one denies that at times this is difficult, but such difficulties do not make periodic abstinence "unnatural." "Natural" means living up to the moral demands of our human nature, a nature "created in the image and likeness of God." All of the Ten Commandments are sometimes difficult to follow, but all of them spell out the challenge of being true to our own human nature.

Does NFP require extended periods of abstinence?

Usually not. Some couples may have only a week of abstinence per cycle; the average seems to be 9 or 10 days, and most couples will not have more than the 12 to 14 day period of abstinence that has been practiced by Orthodox Jews for approximately 3,000 years. With the grace of Christ and the power of the Holy Spirit, many couples find that the abstinence of NFP is not a drawback but rather a definite asset for their growth as a married couple.

How does NFP affect a marriage?

Sexual self-control helps to build the marital relationship, and therefore most couples report that NFP has a positive effect on their marriages. They find that periodic abstinence helps keep their sexual relationship fresh, improves their communication, reduces feelings of being used, and gives them a deeper respect for each other.

In addition, the practice of chaste periodic abstinence helps to develop the same strength of character that is necessary for marital fidelity and lifelong marriage. NFP couples have an extremely low divorce rate. This makes sense because couples who respect the natural moral law, God's order of creation, can expect to enjoy its benefits. The reported experiences of many couples have been confirmed by scientific social studies[3,4] and by informal surveys showing an extremely low divorce rate among couples practicing NFP.[5]

So NFP builds better marriages?

Yes, but not automatically. Couples rarely begin to practice Natural Family Planning out of a desire to improve their marital relationship. However, if they are going to practice NFP harmoniously, they soon find that they have to communicate more fully and creatively with each other. Many are helped by a CCL brochure, *Creative Abstinence.*[6]

Spouses do not ignore each other at times when they choose to avoid sexual relations; rather, they develop non-genital ways of expressing their love and affection which is the art of marital courtship. In short, they keep alive the chaste courtship which before marriage led them to want to marry each other.

Peace of conscience, the absence of feelings of being used, and no fear of the dangerous effects of some unnatural methods also contribute to an improved marital relationship.

Can NFP be misused?

Of course. Every gift of God is misused or abused by some people at least some of the time—good wine, food, sex, and even spouses and children and friends. That's why Pope John Paul II has insisted that the teaching of morality be integrated with the teaching of the natural methods.

> It should be clear that what is of concern here is more than just simple "instruction" divorced from the moral values proper to teaching people about love.[7]

Is NFP just "Catholic birth control" for those who are selfishly closed to life?

No. The Holy Father continued in the same talk to note that proper moral instruction

> allows people to see that it is not possible to practice natural methods as a "licit" variation of the decision to be

closed to life, which would be substantially the same as that which inspires the decision to use contraceptives: only if there is a basic openness to fatherhood and motherhood, understood as collaborating with the Creator, does the use of natural means become an integrating part of the responsibility for love and life.[8]

Should we discuss our "family plans" with a priest?

If you are perplexed as to whether you have sufficiently serious reasons to postpone pregnancy, you might find it very helpful to talk about your situation with the priest or deacon who is helping you prepare for marriage. In my personal opinion, big school debts and the high price of housing in some parts of the country provide some couples with sufficient reasons to postpone pregnancy for a while. But for how long? This gets tricky, and several principles need to be kept in mind.

1. Marriage *is* for family, and you do need a sufficiently serious reason to postpone pregnancy.

2. The longer you plan to postpone pregnancy, the more serious reason you need. For example, it's one thing to postpone pregnancy for three months in order to become more familiar with your signs of fertility. But what if you're thinking in terms of a year or two or more?

3. We are all in danger of having our Christian perspective clouded and warped by the comfortable materialism that surrounds us. It is seductive, and we need help in being true to the Lord, in walking the narrow way with Him, in seeing life with his perspective.

4. An impartial, Christ-centered third party such as a good priest can help us to evaluate our circumstances and our reasoning. Such a priest can also help us to understand if and when we are being too strict with ourselves.

5. Biologically, you may be less fertile a year from now. You may not be able to achieve pregnancy whenever you desire. Some couples have registered extreme disappointment that their NFP teachers did not emphasize this more than they did.

6. In my personal opinion, NFP should be used "with regrets" at the circumstances which lead you to think it would not be responsible for you to seek pregnancy at that particular time.

How can I learn how to practice NFP?

Many parishes, dioceses, and hospitals offer courses in natural family planning, and many of these use the program or the materials of the Couple to Couple League for Natural Family Planning. In addition, the League has an excellent *Home Study Course* for those who cannot attend classes. For further information about the League materials and services, including those in your area, contact CCL at P.O. Box 111184, Cincinnati, OH 45211. Phone: (513) 471-2000. E-mail: ccli@ccli.org. Website: www.ccli.org.

Answer and discuss with your fiance:

1. T   F   Natural Family Planning (NFP) is based on the fact that a woman's body provides certain physical signs which indicate her fertile and infertile times.

2. T   F   Modern NFP methods are much more effective than the "Rhythm Method" developed in the 1930s.

3. T   F   NFP works for women with irregular cycles.

4. T   F   A great benefit of NFP is that it avoids the unhealthy effects of birth control chemicals and devices.

5. T   F   NFP can help couples of marginal fertility to achieve pregnancy.

6. T   F   The divorce rate for couples using NFP is extremely low.

7. T   F   The Church teaches that NFP must not be used selfishly.

References
    1. Maclyn E. Wade, M.D., Phyllis McCarthy, Ph.D., et al., "A randomized prospective study of the use-effectiveness of two methods of natural family planning," *American Journal of Obstetrics and Gynecology*, 15 October 1981, 141:4, 368-376. "There were no method failures in the STM group," 374.
    2. For further information and references, see the brochure "Breastfeeding: Does It Really Space Babies? (Couple to Couple League, 1991). For practical help on how to do ecological breastfeeding in Western culture, see Sheila K. Kippley, *Breastfeeding and Natural Child Spacing: How Ecological Breastfeeding Spaces Babies* (Cincinnati: Couple to Couple League, 1999).
    3. Mary Peter McCusker, *Couples' Perceptions of the Use of Fertility*

Awareness Methods of Natural Family Planning on Their Marriage Relationship (Washington, D.C.: Catholic University of America) A Master's degree thesis, June, 1976.

4. Joseph Tortorici, "Contraception Regulation, Self-Esteem, and Marital Satisfaction among Catholic Couples: Michigan State University Study," *International Review of Natural Family Planning* 3:3 (Fall, 1979) 191-205.

5. One survey showed that less than 1% of responding NFP users had been divorced and remarried. (Nona Aguilar, *No-Pill, No-Risk Birth Control* [New York: Rawson Wade, 1980] 104-105). Priests with long experience in Catholic marriage tribunals have said that in almost all cases of divorce, it has been preceded by unchastity — either contraception during the marriage or by pre-marital sex or both.

6. Oscar and Susan Staudt, "Creative Abstinence," (Couple to Couple League, 1989).

7. "Pope calls spouses to a sense of responsibility for love and life," *L 'Osservatore Romano*, 17 December 1990, 3.

8. "Pope calls spouses . . .," above.

All the quiz answers are true.

10. Finances

The way you handle your money as a married couple can be either a source of bonding or a source of irritation and even alienation. Therefore it's important to discuss finances before you get married. Now, what's critical is not *just* that you *agree* about money matters; after all, two people could agree to a plan that was both silly and untouched by the Gospel. What you need is a budget that is Christian and prudent in the best sense of that word.

This chapter does not attempt to get into the details of budgeting (quite important), the use of credit cards (can be helpful for an emergency but can also be disastrous), savings plans, etc. You can get that help elsewhere, but beware: much of that advice is provided as if the accumulation of money were the goal of life.

Since you are entering Christian marriage, what is more important than to let Christ direct your thinking about life, including finances? The gospels show us that Jesus definitely taught about money and wealth, and the opinions expressed in this chapter are an effort to apply that teaching to the economic aspects of marriage.

What did Jesus teach about money and wealth?

The Gospel of Luke is particularly revealing about the teachings of Jesus about money and wealth, for Luke has at least ten passages which convey the attitude and doctrine of Christ.

1. Jesus was born in the extremely humble surroundings of a cave in the little town of Bethlehem (Lk 2:1-20). Isn't that teaching by example?

2. Similarly, He noted that "Foxes have holes, and birds of the air have nests, but the Son of Man has nowhere to lay his head" (Lk 9:57).

3. In the gospel of Matthew, we read, "Blessed are the poor in spirit, for theirs is the kingdom of God" (Mt 5:3). In Luke, however, we read, "Blessed are you poor, for yours is the kingdom of God" (6:20). Furthermore, Luke follows the beatitudes with opposing woes: "But woe to you that are rich, for you have received your consolation" (6:24).

4. Chapter 12 of Luke contains four separate but related sayings of Jesus about wealth.

Jesus starts the parable of the two barns by teaching, "Take heed, and beware of all covetousness; for a man's life does not consist in the abundance of his possessions." He illustrates this with the story of the man who had so much that he was going to pull down his barns and build larger ones, saying to himself,

> "Soul, you have ample goods laid up for many years; take your ease, eat drink and be merry." But God said to him, "Fool! This night your soul is required of you; and the things you have prepared, whose will they be?" So is he who lays up treasures for himself, and is not rich toward God" (Lk 12:13-22).

5. The Lord then continued with the story of the lilies of the field which He concluded with this teaching:

> "Do not seek what you are to eat and what you are to drink, nor be of anxious mind. For all the nations of the world seek these things; and your Father knows that you need them. Instead, seek his kingdom, and these things shall be yours as well" (Lk 12:29-31).

6. Next Jesus teaches us to build up treasures in heaven:

> "Fear not, little flock, for it is your Father's good pleasure to give you the kingdom. Sell your possessions, and give alms; provide yourselves with purses that do not grow old, with a treasure in the heavens that does not fail, where no thief approaches and no moth destroys. For where your treasure is, there will your heart be also" (Lk 12:32-34).

7. Chapter 16 in Luke contains two parables which illustrate the teaching of Jesus about money and wealth. ("Mammon" is generally interpreted as money.) At the conclusion of the parable of the unjust steward, He says,

> "No servant can serve two masters; for either he will hate the one and love the other; or he will be devoted to the one and despise the other. You cannot serve God and mammon" (Lk 16:13).

8. A powerful image of the dangers of wealth is provided in the story of the rich man and the poor beggar, Lazarus, a man

> "full of sores who desired to be fed with what fell from the rich man's table; moreover, the dogs came and licked his sores. The poor man died and was carried by the angels to Abraham's bosom. The rich man also died and was buried; and in Hades, being in torment, he lifted up his eyes, and saw Abraham far off and Lazarus in his bosom" (Lk 16:19-31).

9. The account about the rich man who was keeping all the command-ments is generally used to illustrate the value of the vow of poverty for those who follow Jesus in the life of dedicated religious service. However, the conclusion also serves our purpose of showing the attitude and teaching of Jesus about money and possessions.

> "One thing you still lack. Sell all that you have and distribute to the poor, and you will have treasure in heaven, and come, follow me." But when he heard this he became sad, for he was very rich. Jesus looking at him said, "How hard it is for those who have riches to enter the Kingdom of God! For it easier for a camel to go through the eye of a needle than for a rich man to enter the kingdom of God." Those who heard it said, "Then who can be saved?' But He said, "What is impossible with men is possible with God" (Lk 18:18-27).

10. Some people tell themselves that later, when they have a lot more money, they will contribute generously to the support of the Church. Jesus teaches about the value of giving a fair share of what we have now.

> He looked up and saw the rich putting their gifts into the treasury; and He saw a poor widow put in two copper coins. And He said, "Truly, I tell you, this poor widow has put in more than all of them; for they all contributed out of their abundance, but she out of her poverty put in all the living that she had" (Lk 21:1-4).

In brief, while there is nothing wrong in wanting to have a responsible job which pays well, the idea of accumulating wealth for the sake of wealth runs completely contrary to the teachings of Jesus. Possessions and even your earning abilities should be regarded as a matter for stewardship.

What is Christian stewardship?

Christian stewardship is first an attitude which recognizes the Lord's dominion over our lives. With that attitude you ask, "What do I have that I have not received from others and ultimately from the Lord? Good health? A sound mind and a certain level of intelligence? Parents who cared for me and educated me? Children? Any special talents? An inheritance? The ability to work productively and earn a living?"

With the attitude of stewardship, the Christian asks further, "How am I to share with others the goods that the Lord has shared with me?"

What is tithing?

Tithing is a form of stewardship of one's income. It means literally to give a tenth of one's income back to the Lord, and it has its roots in the Old Testament (Deut 14:22f). The idea is to give back to the Lord "off the top," not just the leftovers, in thanksgiving for all that you have been able to earn, for without his gifts of mind and health and talents, how much would you have been able to earn?

How much of your income is really income? In my opinion, gross income is something you never see, so you should deduct all the taxes you pay, including social security to arrive at your basis for tithing.

What percentage should you tithe? I know that many interpret the biblical tithe as less than a tenth, but who am I to suggest less than what Scripture describes? And who am I to say that those who are in the upper income categories should limit themselves to a tenth?

To what works should you distribute your tithe?

If you are Catholic, normally your parish church should be a prime beneficiary of your tithing because the parish is the front line of the spiritual services of the Church. Good priests need and deserve your support. Other beneficiaries of your tithing should be organizations which are doing the works of the Lord.

How much should we spend on our wedding and reception?

The actual cost of having your marriage vows witnessed by a priest and two witnesses is almost nothing. What runs up the costs are all those things which are not essential to the Sacrament of Matrimony.

The wedding gown? My bride made her own in 1963; I know of another young woman whose wealthy parents spent about $2,500 (1990 dollars) on the dress. A few days or weeks later, who's going to remember the details of finery that can really run up the costs?

The reception? I've been to dozens ranging from full service sit-down hotel dinners to the more typical wedding hall cafeteria style meals, and I can tell you that by the time you return from your honeymoon, almost no one will remember anything special about your wedding and reception unless somebody goofs—like the father who introduced all the members of the wedding party but forgot the bride and groom. A personal note: if it's the custom in your area to have torchy strip-tease music for the garter bit, dare to be different; just skip the whole garter thing. That music and the accompanying actions have always seemed out of place at a celebration of chaste marriage.

How much money do you need to start your married life together?

Normally, the most important thing is sufficient employment to cover the basics of family life — charity, clothing, food, housing, dental and medical care, transportation, utilities, and usually some insurance. It may be that some who are at the low end of the economic ladder need to give more thought to what it is actually going to cost to be a family unit; on the other hand, others may give far too much consideration to the economics of family life and use this as an excuse for postponing both their first baby and for severely limiting the size of their family.

What if we have big debts when we marry?

Discuss the size of your respective debts before you marry. If you have big debts simply from overspending, you're in trouble, and you had better start living by a budget or you are going to have many a problem in your life together. If you have educational debts, work up a repayment schedule. If you will have two incomes till your first baby, try to dedicate the entirety of the *higher* income to debt repayment.

What sort of goods do we need when we first get married?

One of the most important lessons we all have to learn is to distinguish between wants and needs. What you actually need by way of material goods to start life together is actually very little. A kitchen table and two to four chairs and minimum eating and cooking utensils. A few things to sit on in the living room. Something to sleep on and something to put your clothes in. That's it.

What sort of things *don't* we need when we're newly married?

Many newlyweds invest large sums of money and incur big debts for furniture for which they have no real need. You don't need a headboard and footboard on your bed. You don't need a suite of expensive bedroom furniture. You don't need an expensive dining room set or expensive living room pieces. Besides, your tastes may change considerably. It's much more important to pay off your school debts, if you have any, than to invest in furniture that you may regret owning in a few years — especially if you have to move a few times. It's amazing how much good stuff you can get by shopping the want-ads, the estate sales, and the yard sales.

Also very big on the list of what you do not need when you get married is a house, especially a large one. And if and when you do buy a house, does it make Christian sense to get one that's going to require two incomes to make the mortgage payments? Please remember: marriage is for family, and the childhood development experts agree: kids need a full-time mom around the house.[1]

What's really important in all this?

What's really important in your preparations for marriage—and throughout your years of married life—is to keep in the forefront of your minds that you are entering (or have entered) **Christian** marriage. You are saying that you accept Jesus as your Lord and Savior, that you recognize that walking with Him in this life is imperative for living with Him for all eternity. Then be sure to let Him walk with you as you prepare for marriage, as you celebrate your marriage, and as you raise your family. As St. Paul put it, "Put on the Lord Jesus Christ" (Rom 13:14). Let his mind and heart and attitudes become your mind and heart and attitudes. Let your married life together be one of Christian discipleship in the material things of life as well as in the bedroom and on Sunday morning.

Truly Christian stewardship of your resources will be a source of marital bonding. However, unchristian attitudes and handling of your money may well leave you with feelings of uneasiness at best or stress, conflict, and tension.

Discuss with your fiance:

1. This chapter cited several passages of Scripture concerning what Jesus taught about money and wealth. Discuss what these passages teach you.

2. What is Christian stewardship and how will you both implement it in your marriage?

3. What is the difference between "wants" and "needs"? Discuss the "needs" you anticipate when you first get married. Discuss the "wants" that may have to wait.

References

1. "The First Three Years: the importance of mother/child togetherness" (Cincinnati, Box 111184, 45211: Foundation for the Family, 1988) leaflet. See also "The Crucial First Three Years," an 18-page booklet by Sheila Matgen Kippley (Cincinnati, Box 111184, 45211: Couple to Couple League, 1998).

11. The Wedding

The day of the wedding is truly a great day in the life of a married couple for it marks the beginning of a whole new life—their life together as husband and wife, not just as two individuals. To those who understand what marriage is all about, it is a time of celebration because two people are making a public profession of their promises to be husband and wife until death parts them, to exercise caring love for better and for worse. It is a tremendous commitment. It always has been, but in most of Christian history, the couple would find widespread social support for their marriage, while today the State no-fault divorce laws are eroding that support. It is indeed a cause for celebration that you and your fiance are joining with God to create this lifelong bond between you.

Should we try to make our wedding ceremony unique?

Your wedding is unique because you and your beloved are getting married. There is no need to try to make your wedding unique in other respects. I have been to many weddings, and after a few of them, they all become blurred in memory; the only things that stand out are the occasional and always somewhat humorous gaffes, the things that didn't go according to plan. So instead of tying yourselves in knots with all sorts of elaborate preparations for details that almost no one will appreciate or remember, my personal suggestion would be to keep it simple and relaxed; enjoy life in those last weeks before the wedding, and enjoy your wedding and reception.

How do we work with the priest who will be celebrating our wedding?

Ask but do not tell. That is, do not approach the priest with a list of demands. Your priest wants your wedding to be a happy moment for everyone. He also wants the preparations to be pleasant. He has most likely had considerable experience in the celebration of weddings, and he is also under the constraints of ecclesiastical law regarding liturgical celebrations. Make good use of his experience. If you have questions about anything connected with the ceremonies, ask, and he will be pleased to give you an answer.

Can we select the readings at the wedding Mass?

Yes, within certain limits. All readings must be from Sacred Scripture, and you can choose from the following wide variety of biblical passages.

Old Testament Reading
Genesis 1: 26-28, 31
Genesis 2:18-24
Genesis 24:48-51, 58-67
Tobit 7:6-14
Tobit 8:4b-8
Proverbs 31:10-13, 19-20, 30-31
Song of Songs 2:8-10, 14, 16a; 8:6-7
Sirach 26:1-4, 13-16
Jeremiah 31:31-32a, 33-34a

New Testament Reading
Romans 8:31b-35, 37-39
Romans 12:1-2, 9-18 or 12:1-2, 9-13
Romans 15:1b-3a, 5-7, 13
1 Corinthians 6:13c-15a, 17-20
1 Corinthians 12:31-13:8a
Ephesians 5:2a, 21-33 or 5:2a, 25-32
Philippians 4:4-9
Colossians 3:12-17
Hebrews 13:1-4a, 5-6b
1 Peter 3:1-9
1 John 3:18-24
1 John 4:7-12
Revelation 19:1, 5-9a

Responsorial Psalm
Psalm 33:12, 18, 20-21, 22
Psalm 34:2-3, 4-5, 6-7, 8-9
Psalm 103:1-2, 8, 13, 17-18a
Psalm 112:1bc-2, 3-4, 5-7a, 7b-8, 9
Psalm 128:1-2, 3, 4-5
Psalm 145:8-9, 10, 15, 17-18
Psalm 148:1-2, 3-4, 9-10, 11-13a, 13c-14a

Verse before the Gospel
1 John 4:7b
1 John 4:8b, 11
1 John 4:12
1 John 4:16

The Gospel
Matthew 5:1-12a
Matthew 5:13-16
Matthew 7:21, 24-29 or 7:21, 24-25
Matthew 19:3-6
Matthew 22:35-40
Mark 10:6-9
John 2:1-11
John 15:9-12
John 15:12-16
John 17:20-26 or 17:20-23

Can we select any music we desire?

Be sure to ask your priest or parish music director this question; the answer may be different in various dioceses. In general, music in the Liturgy is supposed to be both sacred and art; secular selections are limited to the time before the opening of Mass if allowed at all.

The important thing to remember is that you are assisting your priest in planning a sacred ceremony; the music should be such that it assists your friends and relatives to lift up their minds and hearts to God because that's the general purpose of all sacred music. And if they do lift their minds to God, it is likely they will be praying for you, the bride and groom.

You can direct the musician at your reception to play exactly what you want by way of secular music; you do not need to go along with his or her standard repertoire, and you would do well to find out well ahead of time what the disk jockey or band will be playing in case you don't specify it. You can also discuss the level of volume ahead of time to make sure that you are in control. You should decide ahead of time whether you want your guests to be able to talk with each other while music is playing or if conversation will be made all but impossible by high volume; and you might do well to discuss this ahead of time with your parents.

Should we have the Rite of Christian Marriage inside or outside of Mass?

This is certainly something to discuss with your priest. It is traditional for the Catholic bride and groom to exchange their vows in the context of the Holy Sacrifice of the Mass because that symbolizes the placement of your marriage in the context of Christian discipleship. It is important to realize, however, that you are just as "married" if you have the Rite of Christian

Marriage outside of Mass.

If one of you is not Catholic but a baptized Christian, the marriage may take place during Mass although Holy Communion can be given only to those who are practicing Catholics. If the bride or groom who is not Catholic is also not a baptized Christian, the marriage ordinarily may not take place during Mass.

A key issue is whether both families are Catholic. A related issue is whether the parents of the bridal couple are still married to their original spouses or are divorced and remarried. I am not saying that any of these issues makes it impossible to celebrate the Rite of Christian Marriage within a wedding Mass, but they are factors that you will want to discuss with your priest in arriving at a decision.

Furthermore, if a couple are having sexual relations before marriage and are unrepentant, then it would seem hypocritical and even sacrilegious to place their promises in the context of celebrating the saving work of Christ. Such a couple should not receive Holy Communion until they are truly repentant and have been to confession for the Sacrament of Reconciliation.

Should the bride lay a bouquet of flowers at the feet of a statue of our Blessed Mother?

This is not part of the official Catholic ceremony, but it is a beautiful tradition in many churches which have such statues. It symbolizes a devotion to Mary and the recognition of need for her help to be pure and faithful in marriage. However, if the wedding couple intend to start their marriage with unnatural forms of birth control, then they are deciding to live in marital impurity. In such circumstances, is it right for the bride to pretend that she is really putting their lives under the special protection of the Virgin Mary?

What about other ceremonies such as the lighting of symbolic candles, etc.?

Again, these are not part of the official Catholic rite of marriage. If you are thinking about any such ceremonies, be sure to discuss this question with your priest to find out if they are permissible. And, of course, talk over the symbolism of each particular ceremony.

Are there any Church regulations about the wedding clothes?

There's nothing specific, but the general norms of modesty still apply. Many young women have no idea what effect they have on men when they

104

reveal a good portion of their breasts or wear short skirts or tight pants which focus visual attention upon their bodies. They provide completely unnecessary temptations to many men, and that's what is meant by immodest dress.

Judging from what I have seen, it would seem that some young brides are either unaware of the norms of modesty or are ignoring them. I know of at least one priest who makes it clear to each prospective bride that he will not officiate at her wedding if she wears a revealing dress. If you stop to think about it, there's no reason why a priest should have to look down a cleavage while he is officiating at what is supposed to be the beginning of a chaste and holy marriage.

Who should pay for the wedding and the reception?

There is no right or wrong answer to this question. Despite what the wedding etiquette books may say, when it comes to the finances of a wedding and the reception, nothing is cut in stone. Therefore, it is extremely important for you to discuss these matters well ahead of time with your parents.

While it is — or has been — customary in the United States for the parents of the bride to pay for the wedding and the reception, much will depend in actual practice upon the financial resources of your parents as well as local custom. (In some cultures, it's exactly the opposite: the groom's family pays a "bride price," sometimes very high, to the parents of the bride.) Many parents set a definite limit to the amount of their financial contribution; anything over that amount has to be taken care of by the bride and groom, both of whom are frequently working.

Additional financial complications come in when the bride comes from a family of modest income and marries a man from a wealthy family which wants to invite many guests to the reception. In such cases, the notion of the bride's family taking care of the wedding and reception would seem definitely inappropriate, and it would seem that there should be some frank negotiations. Perhaps the wealthy family would want to pay for all the expenses or at least their guests' share.

The marital status of the parents of the bridal couple can greatly affect the financial arrangements. Divorce can definitely influence how a given parent feels about financial affairs, and this might be even more difficult or touchy when one or more of such parents has remarried.

When should we discuss these various matters, especially those which might be difficult?

The shadow of unresolved problems (or things that *might* be problems) can dim the whole period of preparation for marriage. Therefore, I would suggest an early discussion of all the wedding and reception plans. Another suggestion would be that you not enter into such discussions with your minds already made up about things that are negotiable. You may learn something from those with more experience, and you may find that certain realities will cause you to change your tentative plans—so keep them tentative.

Discuss with your fiance:

During your marriage ceremony, you are coming before God to make a lifelong commitment. How will this affect such things as the elaborateness or simplicity of the wedding details? the music you choose for the wedding? the attire of the wedding party?

12. The Honeymoon

It seems to me that the honeymoon experience will be entirely different for different groups of couples. For those who have practiced premarital chastity, it can be a time of never-before sexual intimacy. For those who have not been chaste before marriage — especially if they have been living together or fornicating on their dates, it will be much less, perhaps just another vacation.

For those who are entering marriage with the intention of postponing pregnancy for a while, there are other questions about marital chastity.

Then, there are questions about what sort of honeymoon to take and when to take it.

Lastly, don't be surprised if the honeymoon and the next few weeks provide you with an opportunity to use some of those communication skills mentioned in Chapter 7. Melding two independent lives into one married life will most likely require some changes from both spouses, changes are occasions for stress, and handling stress properly calls for good communication.

When should we take our honeymoon?

There is no law that says you have to take your honeymoon right after your wedding. Some couples will delay their honeymoon-vacation for a few weeks or a few months for various reasons including the weather in the place they would like to visit.

Where should we go on our honeymoon?

Again, there is no law that says you have to go anywhere. You may live in an area that some people come to for their vacations, but you've never had the time to enjoy the local attractions. You might be surprised at how much there is to see and do within your own city or general locality. There is absolutely no certainty that an expensive trip to an exotic location is going to help you get your marriage off to a better start than a more localized vacation.

What if we have sufficient reason to delay pregnancy but our wedding occurs in the fertile time?

It's not an unusual situation. You have two moral options. Either engage in marital relations and let a baby come if God sees fit to bless you in that way, or abstain until you are infertile. Chaste married couples have done it both ways.

There may be some ways of getting around this "problem." If the prospective bride has a somewhat regular menstrual-fertility cycle, she can try to schedule the wedding so it occurs in an infertile time. Or, if it is quite clear as the wedding approaches that you will be in the fertile time, perhaps you can postpone the honeymoon for a week or so after the wedding. The great advantage of that is that you could get your apartment in good shape, do any gift exchanges, and have all your thank-you notes written before you go on your honeymoon-vacation.

Please, do not start your marriage with contraception, even if only on your honeymoon. It is still the grave matter of mortal sin. It contradicts the very meaning of marriage as a relationship in which you will grow in holiness, cooperating with the graces of the Sacrament of Matrimony. Furthermore, it is a sin that may be very difficult to repent of, for true repentance calls for sorrow and an attitude of "if I had it to do over again, I would not do that sinful action." What I am saying is that if you enjoy a very sensual honeymoon-vacation made easy by contraception, you may have a very hard time telling yourself honestly that if you had it to do over again tomorrow, you wouldn't.

What's the experience of newlyweds who honeymoon during the fertile time?

That question was asked of readers of *CCL Family Foundations*, the mini-magazine of The Couple to Couple League for natural family planning. The following are some of the responses.

Two months before my wedding, my NFP chart enabled me to realize ovulation would probably occur the first day of my honeymoon. Even though I was raised in a large Catholic family endorsing NFP, the possibility of conceiving the first year of marriage deeply bothered me. Much to my surprise, the secularization and materialism plaguing society had, to a degree, penetrated my strong Catholic upbringing regarding children and marriage. Like many engaged couples, I planned to further my career for a couple of years and to acquire the "perfect" house complete with furnishings before conceiving children. The fantasy of a cozy house and a mother who wanted to stay at home because she already spent a few years in the workplace appeared perfect. Obviously, society impressed upon me the thought that newlyweds shouldn't be burdened with children the first year of marriage.

Luckily, God blessed me with a fiance who respected my femininity and encouraged me not to worry about the things I had no power to change. I also had numerous conversations with my mother about this. She totally understood my fear and worked to reassure me. However, as my wedding approached and my cycle remained regular, my nervousness regarding the reality of immediate pregnancy increased dramatically. I simply refused to surrender my dreams for the reality and truth God held for me. My mother rightly replied that if I refused to accept children when God saw fit, then I was incapable of a genuine Catholic marriage.

This honest assessment whipped my faith into shape. After weeks of lamenting the real possibility of conceiving on my honeymoon, I finally left this matter in God's hands.

My husband and I did have relations during our honeymoon, and much to our surprise, we did not conceive. The real irony is that during our second month of marriage, we were so impressed with how we managed not to conceive during the first month's fertile time that we threw all caution to the wind and conceived during this time. Yes, at first we dared to be upset, but after some real soul-searching we both realized that we truly believed children to be a blessing, regardless of how long we were married before conceiving. What prevented us from knowing this truth from the beginning was a self-centered attitude we unknowingly adopted from our secular society which claimed that a couple who waits to bring children into the world is somehow a happier, more mature team.

About 11 months after our wedding, I gave birth to a beautiful daughter. Neither of us can imagine marriage without her.

—*S.R., PA*

It is possible to plan a honeymoon to fall during the infertile time. Just 11 months ago, my wife and I successfully had the infertile time during our honeymoon. Here are some helpful hints in achieving this:

1) Take an NFP course when first engaged. 2) Work on accurate charting; look for cycle trends. 3) Try to schedule the wedding to accommodate your cycle trend (for example, the beginning of the month, the end of the month). 4) If your

honeymoon falls on fertile days, plan many activities outside the bedroom, and enjoy yourselves together. 5) Refrain from purchasing "backup" artificial contraception; it will only weaken your self-control. 6) Pray for strength in maintaining self-control during the fertile time.

One of our most gratifying experiences is celebrating our sexuality on our Creator's terms. My wife and I have been extremely pleased with NFP and the effects it has on our marriage.
— S.P., IN

We were in the fertile time on our honeymoon, but we didn't get pregnant right away either. We abstained. Believe it or not, you don't have to have intercourse on your wedding night.

My husband and I went into our marriage mature enough to know that intercourse on our honeymoon wasn't the first priority. Mutual respect and shared lifetime goals were much more important. Sure, it was hard, but we'd waited our whole lives to give ourselves to each other. What did a couple more weeks matter?
— L. & P.C., MN

When my husband and I were engaged, I had strong feelings to wait a year before getting pregnant. A few months before our wedding day I was calculating whether or not I would be fertile. As the day came closer, I became anxious because I knew my ovulation was being delayed and not following my previous cycle patterns.

What to do on our wedding night? Well, I made my new husband aware of the possibility of pregnancy and we decided to take our chances. We thought maybe it wouldn't happen, plus we were so in love and we wanted to consummate our marriage. We were so happy to be together we thought we would leave it up to God.

A few weeks later I realized I was pregnant. There were mixed emotions of disappointment and happiness that we both talked about. Well, it does take nine months and that gave us plenty of time to get used to the idea and we became very excited and anxious waiting for the birth.

When our son was born on Valentine's Day, there was such a feeling of joy that overwhelmed us that we both cried. I cannot imagine what we would have missed out on if we did not do God's will.

— J.S., OH

My husband and I have been married eight months. We are both born-again Protestants and believe that only NFP works in cooperation with God in the matter of creating life. We accepted early in our engagement that we might have to abstain during part of our honeymoon.

We found out there are many reasons for choosing a wedding date, most of which have nothing to do with your cycle! We chose a date based on relatives, church availability, reception places, etc., and left the rest up to God.

I started my period the day before our wedding. In my case, Phase I lasted for nine days and so we abstained the last six days of our honeymoon. I had thought in advance that I would be terribly disappointed if that happened, because I had waited a long time to get married (I was 30 and a virgin), and by the grace of God and lots of prayer we had been sexually pure during our two-year courtship and engagement. However, God always works benefits into situations where we don't expect them, and I feel since we accepted that there would be abstinence during part of our honeymoon, we focused on other things. We toured a lot around our honeymoon destination (more than we would have if it had been Phase I or III!), we ate out more and had wonderful conversations, we had more time to pray together, we wandered into little book stores and little shops, sat in plazas and had coffee. In other words, we focused on getting to know each other in ways other than the physical, and since we were now married, we felt that we had a gift that we would just wait a little bit longer to unwrap more fully.

Also, while this is something that is hard for an engaged couple to believe, sex in the beginning usually involves a certain amount of stress and work, and if you're a virgin, a little pain. It is not what the movies portray! I think we were relieved of stress and pressure because we had to abstain for a few days.

I would also like to make a strong case for doing everything possible to take two weeks for the honeymoon. You are truly getting to know each other, and what can be more important than feeling unrushed during this time. Also, if you do hit Phase II during that time, you don't feel so much pressure and disappointment since you know it won't last for the entire honeymoon.

My husband and I have learned so much using NFP. We decided a few months ago that we would like a baby. Because of NFP, I knew when I was ovulating and God allowed us to conceive the first month.

— K. S., VA

My husband and I started our marriage four years ago believing in NFP as the only way to live our married life. We took the classes before we were married and through prayer and discussion decided we would postpone starting our family. We discussed the possibility that our honeymoon would end up smack in the middle of Phase II, and decided if it did, we would wait until we were in Phase III to physically celebrate our marriage vows.

As it turned out, I experienced the longest cycle of my life (66 days) due to the stress and excitement of a new home and husband. We prayerfully and anxiously awaited our precious thermal shift for a month after we were married. We finally celebrated our physical union with much love and respect for each other, and with clear consciences.

We truly believe that this is the way to a wonderful Christian marriage — God is in on all our decisions. We are currently in process to become a teaching couple and have a beautiful 13 month-old son who is expecting a brother or sister in June of next year. Our advice is to practice NFP with no reservations, talk to each other, pray together, and put your marriage in God's capable hands.

— J. B. OH

Concerned about getting pregnant on your honeymoon? I say don't worry! Enjoy your honeymoon! If the Lord decides you should conceive, you should be open to his plan for you and trust Him completely. The main purpose of marriage is to bring children into the world.

My sister is the closest friend I have. She conceived on her honeymoon and had a beautiful baby girl nine months later. She always dreamed of having a large family or, as she would say, "as many as the Lord sends me." I even assisted her in purchasing a large table that would sit "at least six children" around it. She has never been able to conceive since, and it has been 10 years.

I have five children (and will also have as many as God sends) and we often talk and sometimes laugh at how we are at different sides of the spectrum. Her longing for more children and loving mine as she does really makes me appreciate and know what blessings children are and how special the gift of fertility is. Maybe if she hadn't conceived on her honeymoon she never would have borne a child.

No matter what our reasons are for postponing pregnancies in our marriages, if it isn't the will of God, it isn't right and will be damaging to the soul. Let us remember why God gave us the sacrament of marriage in the first place and then trust in Him completely, accepting whatever He sends or doesn't send as his will for us.

—I. C., IN

There you have it—a variety of different experiences with one common denominator: the desire to do God's will.

Marriage is the ordinary way in which most people are called to respond to God and to each other and to their children in such a way as to work out their eternal salvation. Pope John Paul II has called the Catholic home "the domestic Church." My prayer for you is that you will always keep in mind that it takes three to get married and that by letting the Lord have his proper place in your marriage, you will grow in faith and in love and thus experience the joys and happiness of a truly Christ-centered marriage and family.

Part II

The Rite of Marriage
and
Readings

The code numbers for the readings (i.e., A-1, B-1, etc.) correspond to The Rite of Marriage Ritual Cards published by Ave Maria Press, Notre Dame, Indiana 46556. The numbers in parentheses refer to the Lectionary numbers when appropriate.

PART II

Rite for Celebrating Marriage During Mass

INTRODUCTORY RITES

Entrance Rite
>Greeting
>Penitential Rite

Opening Prayer

Afterwards the priest, with hands joined, sings or says:
Let us pray.

Priest and people pray silently for a while. Then the priest extends his hands and sings or says the opening prayer, at the end of which the people respond: **Amen.**

A-1	*

Father,
you have made the bond of marriage
a holy mystery,
a symbol of Christ's love for his Church.
Hear our prayers for *N.* **and** *N.*
With faith in you and in each other
they pledge their love today.
May their lives always bear witness
to the reality of that love.

We ask this through our Lord Jesus Christ, your Son,
who lives and reigns with you and the Holy Spirit,
one God, for ever and ever.
R. **Amen.**

---

* *Ave Maria Press Ritual Card number*

A-2

Father,
hear our prayers for N. and N.,
who today are united in marriage before your altar.
Give them your blessing,
and strengthen their love for each other.

We ask this through our Lord Jesus Christ, your Son,
who lives and reigns with you and the Holy Spirit,
one God, for ever and ever.
R. Amen.

A-3

Almighty God,
hear our prayers for N. and N.,
who have come here today
to be united in the sacrament of marriage.
Increase their faith in you and in each other,
and through them bless your Church (with Christian children).

We ask this through our Lord Jesus Christ, your Son,
who lives and reigns with you and the Holy Spirit,
one God, for ever and ever.
R. Amen.

A-4

Father,
when you created mankind
you willed that man and wife should be one.
Bind N. and N.
in the loving union of marriage;
and make their love fruitful
so that they may be living witnesses
to your divine love in the world.

We ask this through our Lord Jesus Christ, your Son,
who lives and reigns with you and the Holy Spirit,
one God, for ever and ever.
R. Amen.

LITURGY OF THE WORD

Note: These readings are taken from the New American Bible.

Old Testament Reading

B-1 * (801-1) **

Genesis 1:26-28, 31a   *Male and female he created them*

A reading from the Book of Genesis

Then God said:
"Let us make man in our image, after our likeness.
Let them have dominion over the fish of the sea,
  the birds of the air, and the cattle,
  and over all the wild animals
  and all the creatures that crawl on the ground."
God created man in his image;
  in the image of God he created him;
  male and female he created them.
God blessed them, saying:
  "Be fertile and multiply;
  fill the earth and subdue it.
Have dominion over the fish of the sea, the birds of the air,
  and all the living things that move on the earth."
God looked at everything he had made, and he found it very good.
The word of the Lord.

B-2 (801-2)

Genesis 2:18-24   *The two of them become one body*

A reading from the Book of Genesis

The LORD God said: "It is not good for the man to be alone.
I will make a suitable partner for him."
So the LORD God formed out of the ground
  various wild animals and various birds of the air,
  and he brought them to the man to see what he would call them;
  whatever the man called each of them would be its name.
The man gave names to all the cattle,

* *Ave Maria Press Ritual Card number*
** *Lectionary number*

117

all the birds of the air, and all wild animals;
but none proved to be the suitable partner for the man.
So the LORD God cast a deep sleep on the man,
 and while he was asleep,
 he took one of his ribs and closed up its place with flesh.
The LORD God then built up into a woman the rib
 that he had taken from the man.
When he brought her to the man, the man said:
 "This one, at last, is bone of my bones
  and flesh of my flesh;
 This one shall be called 'woman',
  for out of 'her man' this one has been taken."
That is why a man leaves his father and mother
 and clings to his wife,
 and the two of them become one body.
The word of the Lord.

B-3 (801-3)

Genesis 24:48-51, 58-67 *In his love for Rebekah, Isaac found solace after the death of his mother.*

A reading from the Book of Genesis
The servant of Abrahm said to Laban:
"I bowed down in worship to the LORD,
 blessing the LORD, the god of my master Abraham,
 who had led me on the right road
 to obtain the daughter of my master's kinsman for his son.
If, therefore, you have in mind to show true loyalty to my master,
 let me know:
 but if not, let me know that, too.
 I can then proceed accordingly."
Laban and his household said in reply:
 "This thing comes from the LORD;
 we can say nothing to you either for or against it.
Here is Rebekah, ready for you;

take her with you,
that she may become the wife of your master's son,
as the LORD has said."
So they called Rebekah and asked her,
"Do you wish to go with this man?"
She answered, "I do."
At this they allowed their sister Rebekah and her nurse to take leave,
along with Abraham's servant and his men.
Invoking a blessing on Rebekah, they said;

"Sister, may you grow
into thousands of myriads;
And may your descendants gain possession
of the gates of their enemies!"

Then Rebekah and her maids started out;
they mounted their camels and followed the man.
So the servant took Rebekah and went on his way.

Meanwhile Isaac had gone from Beer-lahai-roi
and was living in the region of the Negeb.
One day toward evening he went out... in the field,
and as he looked around, he noticed that camels were approaching.
Rebekah, too, was looking about, and when she saw him,
she alighted from her camel and asked the servant,
"Who is the man out there, walking through the fields toward us?"
"That is my master," replied the servant.
Then she covered herself with her veil.

The servant recounted to Isaac all the things he had done.
Then Isaac took Rebekah into his tent;
he married her, and thus she became his wife.
In his love for her, Isaac found solace
after the death of his mother Sarah.
The word of the Lord.

B-4 (801-4)

Tobit 7:6-14 *May the Lord of heaven prosper you both. May he grant you mercy and peace.*

A reading from the Book of Tobit

Raphael and Tobiah entered the house of Raguel and greeted him.
Raguel sprang up and kissed Tobiah, shedding tears of joy.
But when he heard that Tobit had lost his eyesight,
    he was grieved and wept aloud.
He said to Tobiah:
    "My child, God bless you!
You are the son of a noble and good father.
But what a terrible misfortune
    that such a righteous and charitable man
    should be afflicted with blindness!"
He continued to weep in the arms of his kinsman Tobiah.
His wife Edna also wept for Tobit;
    and even their daughter Sarah began to weep.
Afterward, Raguel slaughtered a ram from the flock
    and gave them a cordial reception.
When they had bathed and reclined to eat,
    Tobiah said to Raphael, "Brother Azariah,
    ask Raguel to let me marry my kinswoman Sarah."
Raguel overheard the words;
    so he said to the boy:
    "Eat and drink and be merry tonight,
    for no man is more entitled to marry my daughter Sarah
    than you, brother.
Besides, not even I have the right to give her to anyone but you,
    because you are my closest relative.
But I will explain the situation to you very frankly.
I have given her in marriage to seven men,
    all of whom were kinsmen of ours,
    and all died on the very night they approached her.
But now, son, eat and drink.
I am sure the Lord will look after you both."

Tobiah answered, "I will eat or drink nothing
  until you set aside what belongs to me."
Raguel said to him: "I will do it.
She is yours according to the decree of the Book of Moses.
Your marriage to her has been decided in heaven!
Take your kinswoman;
  From now on you are her love,
  and she is your beloved.
She is yours today and every after.
And tonight, son, may the Lord of heaven prosper you both.
May he grant you mercy and peace."
Then Raguel called his daughter Sarah, and she came to him.
He took her by the hand and gave her to Tobiah with the words:
  "Take her according to the law.
According to the decree written in the Book of Moses she is your wife.
Take her and bring her back safely to your father.
And may the God of heaven grant both of you peace and prosperity."
He then called her mother and told her to bring a scroll,
  so that he might draw up a marriage contract
  stating that he gave Sarah to Tobiah as his wife
  according to the decree of the Mosaic law.
Her mother brought the scroll,
  and he drew up the contact,
  to which they affixed their seals.
Afterward they began to eat and drink.
The word of the Lord.

B-5 (801-5)

Tobit 8:4b-8   *Allow us to live together to a happy old age.*

A reading from the Book of Tobit

On their wedding night Tobiah arose from bed and said to his wife,
  "Sister, get up. Let us pray and beg our Lord
  to have mercy on us and to grant us deliverance."
Sarah got up, and they started to pray
  and beg that deliverance might be theirs.

They began with these words:

"Blessed are you, O God of our fathers;
    praised be your name forever and ever.
Let the heavens and all your creation
    praise you forever.
You made Adam and you gave him his wife Eve
    to be his help and support;
    and from these two the human race descended.
You said, "It is not good for the man to be alone;
    let us make him a partner like himself.'
Now, Lord, you know that I take this wife of mine
    not because of lust,
    but for a noble purpose.
Call down your mercy on me and on her,
    and allow us to live together to a happy old age."

They said together, "Amen, amen."

The word of the Lord.

B-6 (801-6)

Proverbs 31:10-13, 19-20, 30-31 *The woman who fears the Lord is to be praised.*

A reading from the Book of Proverbs

When one finds a worthy wife,
    her value is far beyond pearls.
Her husband, entrusting his heart to her,
    has an unfailing prize.
She brings him good, and not evil
    all the days of her life.
She obtains wool and flax
    and makes cloth with skillful hands.
She puts her hands to the distaff,
    and her fingers ply the spindle.
She reaches out her hands to the poor,
    and extends her arms to the needy.

Charm is deceptive and beauty fleeting;
    the woman who fears the LORD is to be praised.
Give her a reward of her labors,
    and let her works praise her at the city gates.
The word of the Lord.

B-7 (801-7)

Song of Songs 2:8-10, 14, 16a; 8:6-7a   *Stern as death is love.*

A reading from the Song of Songs
Hark! My lover — here he comes
    Springing across the mountains,
    leaping across the hills.
My lover is like a gazelle
    or a young stag.
Here he stands behind our wall,
    gazing through the windows,
    peering through the lattices.
My lover speaks; he says to me,
    "Arise, my beloved, my dove, my beautiful one, and come!
"O my dove in the clefts of the rock,
    in the secret recesses of the cliff,
Let me see you,
    let me hear your voice,
For your voice is sweet,
    and you are lovely."
My lover belongs to me and I to him.
    He says to me:
"Set me as a seal on your heart,
    as a seal on your arm;
For stern as death is love,
    relentless as the nether-world is devotion;
    its flames are a blazing fire.
Deep waters cannot quench love,
    nor floods sweep it away."
The word of the Lord.

B-8 (801-8)

Sirach 26: 1-4, 13-16   *Like the sun rising in the LORD's heavens, the beauty of a virtuous wife is the radiance of her home.*

A reading from the Book of Sirach

Blessed the husband of a good wife,
   twice lengthened are his days;
A worthy wife brings joy to her husband,
   peaceful and full is his life.
A good wife is a generous gift
   bestowed upon him who fears the LORD;
Be he rich or poor, his heart is content,
   and a smile is ever on his face.
A gracious wife delights her husband,
   her thoughtfulness puts flesh on his bones;
A gift from the LORD is her governed speech,
   and her firm virtue is of surpassing worth.
Choicest of blessings is a modest wife,
   priceless her chaste soul.
A holy and decent woman adds grace upon grace;
   indeed, no price is worthy of her temperate soul.
Like the sun rising in the LORD's heavens,
   the beauty of a virtuous wife is the radiance of her home.
The word of the Lord.

B-9 (801-9)

Jeremiah 31:31-32a, 33-34a   *I will make a new covenant with the house of Israel and the house of Judah.*

A reading from the Book of the Prophet Jeremiah
The days are coming, says the LORD,
   when I will make a new covenant with the house of Israel
   and the house of Judah.

124

It will not be like the covenant I made with their fathers:
    the day I took them by the hand
    to lead them forth from the land of Egypt.
But this is the covenant which I will make
    with the house of Israel after those days, says the LORD.
I will place my law within them, and write it upon their hearts;
    I will be their God, and they shall be my people.
No longer will they have need to teach their friends and relatives
    how to know the LORD.
All, from least to greatest, shall know me, says the LORD.
The word of the Lord.

Responsorial Psalm

C-1 (803-1)

Psalm 33:12 and 18, 20-21, 22

> *R.* (5b) The earth is full of the goodness of the Lord.

Blessed is the nation whose God is the LORD,
    the people he has chosen for his own inheritance.
But see, the eyes of the LORD are upon those who fear him,
    upon those who hope for his kindness.

> *R.* The earth is full of the goodness of the Lord.

Our soul waits for the LORD;
    who is our help and our shield.
For in him our hearts rejoice,
    in his holy name we trust.

> *R.* The earth is full of the goodness of the Lord.

May your kindness, O LORD, be upon us,
    who have put our hope in you.

> *R.* The earth is full of the goodness of the Lord.

125

C-2 (803-2)

Psalm 34:2-3, 4-5, 6-7, 8-9

> *R.* (2a) I will bless the Lord at all times.
> *Or: R.* (9a) Taste and see the goodness of the Lord.

I will bless the LORD at all times;
  his praise shall be ever in my mouth.
Let my soul glory in the LORD;
  the lowly will hear me and be glad.

> *R.* I will bless the Lord at all times.
> *Or: R.* Taste and see the goodness of the Lord.

Glorify the LORD with me,
  let us together extol his name.
I sought the LORD, and he answered me,
  and delivered me from all my fears.

> *R.* I will bless the Lord at all times.
> *Or: R.* Taste and see the goodness of the Lord.

Look to him that you may be radiant with joy;
  and your faces may not blush with shame.
When the poor one called out, the LORD heard,
  and from all his distress he saved him.

> *R.* I will bless the Lord at all times.
> *Or: R.* Taste and see the goodness of the Lord.

The angel of the LORD encamps
  around those who fear him, and delivers them.
Taste and see how good the LORD is;
  blessed the man who takes refuge in him.

> *R.* I will bless the Lord at all times.
> *Or: R.* Taste and see the goodness of the Lord.

C-3 (803-3)

Psalm 103:1-2, 8 and 13, 17-18a

> *R.* (8a) The Lord is kind and merciful.
> *Or: R.* (see 17) The Lord's kindness is everlasting to those who fear him.

Bless the LORD, O my soul;
  and all my being, bless his holy name.
Bless the LORD, O my soul,
  and forget not all his benefits.

> *R.* The Lord is kind and merciful.
> *Or: R.* The Lord's kindness is everlasting to those who fear him.

Merciful and gracious is the LORD,
  slow to anger and abounding in kindness.
As a father has compassion on his children,
  so the LORD has compassion on those who fear him.

> *R.* The Lord is kind and merciful.
> *Or: R.* The Lord's kindness is everlasting to those who fear him.

But the kindness of the LORD is from eternity
  to eternity toward those who fear him,
And his justice towards children's children,
  among those who keep his covenant.

> *R.* The Lord is kind and merciful.
> *Or: R.* The Lord's kindness is everlasting to those who fear him.

C-4 (803-4)

Psalm 112:1bc-2, 3-4, 5-7a, 7b-8, 9

> *R.* (see 1) Blessed the man who greatly delights in the Lord's commands.
> *Or: R.* Alleluia.

Blessed the man who fears the LORD,
  who greatly delights in his commands.

His posterity shall be mighty upon the earth;
   the upright generation shall be blessed.

R. **Blessed the man who greatly delights in the Lord's commands.**
Or: R. **Alleluia.**

Wealth and riches shall be in his house;
   his generosity shall endure forever.
Light shines through the darkness for the upright;
   he is gracious and merciful and just.

R. **Blessed the man who greatly delights in the Lord's commands.**
Or: R. **Alleluia.**

Well for the man who is gracious and lends,
   who conducts his affairs with justice;
He shall never be moved;
   the just one shall be in everlasting remembrance.
An evil report he shall not fear.

R. **Blessed the man who greatly delights in the Lord's commands.**
Or: R. **Alleluia.**

His heart is firm, trusting in the LORD.
His heart is steadfast; he shall not fear.
   till he looks down upon his foes.

R. **Blessed the man who greatly delights in the Lord's commands.**
Or: R. **Alleluia.**

Lavishly he gives to the poor;
   his generosity shall endure forever;
   his horn shall be exalted in glory.

R. **Blessed the man who greatly delights in the Lord's commands.**
Or: R. **Alleluia.**

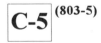 **(803-5)**

Psalm 112:1-2, 3, 4-5

R. **(see 1a) Blessed are those who fear the Lord.**
Or: R. **(4) See how the Lord blesses those who fear him.**

Blessed are you who fear the LORD,
who walk in his ways!
For you shall eat the fruit of your handiwork;
blessed shall you be, and favored.

R. Blessed are those who fear the Lord.
Or: R. **See how the Lord blesses those who fear him.**

Your wife shall be like a fruitful vine
in the recesses of your home;
Your children like olive plants
around your table.

R. Blessed are those who fear the Lord.
Or: R. **See how the Lord blesses those who fear him.**

Behold, thus is the man blessed
who fears the LORD.
The LORD bless you from Zion:
may you see the prosperity of Jerusalem
all the days of your life.

R. Blessed are those who fear the Lord.
Or: R. **See how the Lord blesses those who fear him.**

 C-6 (801-6)

Psalm 145:8-9, 10 and 15, 17-18

R. (9a) The Lord is compassionate toward all his works.

The LORD is gracious and merciful,
slow to anger and of great kindness.
The LORD is good to all,
and compassionate toward all his works.

R. The Lord is compassionate toward all his works.

Let all your works give you thanks, O LORD,
and let your faithful ones bless you.
The eyes of all look hopefully to you
and you give them their food in due season.

R. The Lord is compassionate toward all his works.

The LORD is just in all his ways,
  and holy in all his works.
The LORD is near to all who call upon him,
  to all who call upon him in truth.
R. **The Lord is compassionate toward all his works.**

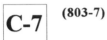 **(803-7)**

Psalm 148:1-2, 3-4, 9-10, 11-13a, 13c-14a

> *R.* **(13a) Let all praise the name of the Lord.**
> *Or: R.* **Alleluia.**

Alleluia.
Praise the LORD from the heavens,
  praise him in the heights;
Praise him, all you his angels,
  praise him, all you his hosts.

> *R.* **Let all praise the name of the Lord.**
> *Or: R.* **Alleluia.**

Praise him, sun and moon;
  praise him, all you shining stars.
Praise him, you highest heavens,
  and you waters above the heavens.

> *R.* **Let all praise the name of the Lord.**
> *Or: R.* **Alleluia.**

You mountains and all you hills,
  you fruit trees and all you cedars;
You wild beasts and all tame animals,
  you creeping things and winged fowl.

> *R.* **Let all praise the name of the Lord.**
> *Or: R.* **Alleluia.**

Let the kings of the earth and all peoples,
  the princes and all the judges of the earth,

Young men too, and maidens,
  old men and boys,
Praise the name of the LORD,
  for his name alone is exalted.

R. **Let all praise the name of the Lord.**
Or: R. **Alleluia.**

His majesty is above earth and heaven,
  and he has lifted his horn above the people.

R. **Let all praise the name of the Lord.**
Or: R. **Alleluia.**

New Testament Reading

D-1	(802-1)

Romans 8:31b-35, 37-39 *What will separate us from the love of Christ?*

A reading from the Letter of Saint Paul to the Romans

Brothers and sisters:
If God is for us, who can be against us?
He did not spare his own Son
  but handed him over for us all,
  will he not also give us everything else along with him?
It is God who acquits us.
Who will condemn?
It is Christ Jesus who died, rather, was raised,
  who also is at the right hand of God,
 who indeed intercedes for us.
What will separate us from the love of Christ?
Will anguish, or distress, or persecution, or famine,
  or nakedness, or peril, or the sword?

No, in all these things, we conquer overwhelmingly
  through him who loved us.

For I am convinced that neither death, nor life,
    nor angels, nor principalities,
    nor present things, nor future things,
    nor powers, nor height, nor depth,
    nor any other creature will be able to separate us
    from the love of God in Christ Jesus our Lord.

The word of the Lord.

 (802-2)

Long Form

Romans 12: 1-2, 9-18 *Offer your bodies as a living sacrifice, holy and pleasing to God.*

A reading from the Letter of Saint Paul to the Romans

I urge you, brothers and sisters, by the mercies of God,
    to offer bodies as a living sacrifice,
    holy and pleasing to God, your spiritual worship.
Do not conform yourselves to this age
    but be transformed by the renewal of your mind,
    that you may discern what is the will of God,
    what is good and pleasing and perfect.

Let love be sincere;
    hate what is evil,
    hold on to what is good;
    love one another with mutual affection;
    anticipate one another in showing honor
Do not grow slack in zeal,
    be fervent in spirit,
    serve the Lord.
Rejoice in hope,
    endure in affliction,
    persevere in prayer.
Contribute to the needs of the holy ones,
    exercise hospitality.

Bless those who persecute you,
  bless and do not curse them.
Rejoice with those who rejoice,
  weep with those who weep.
Have the same regard for one another;
  do not be haughty but associate with the lowly;
  do not be wise in your own estimation.
Do not repay anyone evil for evil;
  be concerned for what is noble in the sight of all.
If possible, on your part, live at peace with all.

The word of the Lord.

Or Short Form

Romans 12:1-2, 9-13   *Offer your bodies as a living sacrifice, holy and pleasing to God.*

A reading from the Letter of Saint Paul to the Romans

I urge you, brothers and sisters, by the mercies of God,
  to offer your bodies as a living sacrifice,
  holy and pleasing to God, your spiritual worship.
Do not conform yourselves to this age
  but be transformed by the renewal of your mind,
  that you may discern what is the will of God,
  what is good and pleasing and perfect.

Let love be sincere;
  hate what is evil,
  hold on to what is good;
  love one another with mutual affection;
  anticipate one another in showing honor.
Do not grow slack in zeal,
  be fervent in spirit,
  serve the Lord.
Rejoice in hope,
  endure in affliction,
  persevere in prayer.
Contribute to the needs of the holy ones,
  exercise hospitality.

The word of the Lord.

(802-3)

Romans 15: 1b-3a, 5-7, 13 *Welcome one another as Christ welcomed you.*

A reading from the Letter of Saint Paul to the Romans

Brothers and sisters:
We ought to put up with the failings of the weak and not to please
    ourselves;
  let each of us please our neighbor for the good,
  for building up.
For Christ did not please himself.
May the God of endurance and encouragement
  grant you to think in harmony with one another,
  in keeping with Christ Jesus,
  that with one accord you may with one voice
  glorify the God and Father of our Lord Jesus Christ.

Welcome one another, then, as Christ welcomed you,
  for the glory of God.
May the God of hope fill you with all joy and peace in believing,
  so that you may abound in hope by the power of the Holy Spirit.

The word of the Lord.

 (802-4)

1 Corinthians 6:13c-15a, 17-20 *Your body is a temple of the spirit.*

A reading from the first letter of Saint Paul to the Corinthians

Brothers and sisters:
The body is not for immorality, but for the Lord,
  and the Lord is for the body;
  God raised the Lord and will also raise us by his power.

Do you not know that your bodies are members of Christ?
Whoever is joined to the Lord becomes one spirit with him.
Avoid immorality.

Every other sin a person commits is outside the body,
but the immoral person sins against his own body.
Do you not know that your body
is a temple of the Holy Spirit within you,
whom you have from God, and that you are not your own?
For you have been purchased at a price.
Therefore glorify God in your body.

The word of the Lord.

 (802-5)

1 Corinthians 12:31-13:8a *If I do not have love, I gain nothing.*

A reading from the first Letter of Saint Paul to the Corinthians.

Brothers and sisters:
Strive eagerly for the greatest spiritual gifts.

But I shall show you a still more excellent way.

If I speak in human and angelic tongues
but do not have love,
I am a resounding gong or a clashing cymbal.
And if I have the gift of prophecy
and comprehend all mysteries and all knowledge;
if I have all faith so as to move mountains,
but do not have love, I am nothing.
If I give away everything I own,
and I hand my body over so that I may boast
but do not have love, I gain nothing.

Love is patient, love is kind.
It is not jealous, is not pompous
it is not inflated, it is not rude,
it does not seek its own interests,
it is not quick-tempered, it does not brood over injury, it does not
rejoice over wrongdoing
but rejoices with the truth.

It bears all things, believes all things,
   hopes all things, endures all things.

Love never fails.

The word of the Lord.

 (802-6)

Long form

Ephesians 5:2a. 21-33 *This is a great mystery, but I speak in reference to Christ and the Church.*

A reading from the Letter of Saint Paul to the Ephesians

Brothers and sisters:
Live in love, as Christ loved us
   and handed himself over for us.

Be subordinate to one another out of reverence for Christ.
Wives should be subordinate to their husbands as to the Lord.
For the husband is head of his wife
   just as Christ is head of the Church,
   he himself the savior of the body.
As the Church is subordinate to Christ,
   so wives should be subordinate to their husbands in everything.
Husbands, love your wives
   even as Christ loved the Church
   and handed himself over for her to sanctify her,
   cleansing her by the bath of water with the word,
   that he might present to himself the church in splendor,
   without spot or wrinkle or any such thing,
   that she might be holy and without blemish.
So also husbands should love their wives as their own bodies.
He who loves his wife loves himself.
For no one hates his own flesh
   but rather nourishes anc cherishes it,
    even as Christ does the Church,

because we are members of his Body.

For this reason a man shall leave his father and his mother
and be joined to his wife,
and the two shall become one flesh.

This is a great mystery,
but I speak in reference to Christ and the Church.
In any case, ech one of you should love his wife as himself,
and the wife should respect her husband.

The word of the Lord.

OR Short Form

Ephesians 5:2a, 25-32 *This is a great mystery, but I speak in reference to Christ and the Church.*

A reading from the Letter of Saint Paul to the Ephesians

Brothers and sisters:
Live in love, as Christ loved us
and handed himself over to us

Husbands, love your wives,
even as Christ loved the Church
and handed himself over for her to sanctify her,
cleansing her by the bath of water with the word,
that he might present to himself the Church in splendor,
without spot or wrinkle or any such thing,
that she might be holy and without blemish.
So also husbands should love their wives as their own bodies.
He who loves his wife loves himself.
For no one hates his own flesh
but rather nourishes and cherishes it,
even as Christ does the Church,
because we are members of his Body.

For this reason a man shall leave his father and his mother
and be joined to his wife,
and the two shall become one flesh.

This is a great mystery,
  but I speak in reference to Christ and the Church.
The word of the Lord.

D-7 (802-7)

Philippians 4: 4-9 *The God of peace will be with you.*

A reading from the Letter of Saint Paul to the Phillippians

Brothers and sisters:
Rejoice in the Lord always.
I shall say it again: rejoice!
Your kindness should be known to all.
The Lord is near.
Have no anxiety at all, but in everything,
  by prayer and petition, with thanksgiving,
  make your requests known to God.
Then the peace of God that surpasses all understanding
  will guard your hearts and minds in Christ Jesus.

Finally, brothers and sisters,
  whatever is true, whatever is honorable,
  whatever is just, whatever is pure,
  whatever is lovely, whatever is gracious,
  if there is any excellence
  and if there is anything worthy of praise,
  think about these things.
Keep on doing what you have learned and received
  and heard and seen in me.
Then the God of peace will be with you.

The word of the Lord.

D-8   (802-8)

Colossians 3: 12-17   *And over all these put on love, that is, the bond of perfection.*

A reading from the Letter of Saint Paul to the Colossians

Brothers and sisters:
Put on, as God's chosen ones, holy and beloved,
    heartfelt compassion, kindness, humility, gentleness, and patience,
    bearing with one another and forgiving one another,
    if one has a grievance against another;
    as the Lord has forgiven you, so must you also do.
And over all these put on love,
    that is the bond of perfection.
And let the peace of Christ control your hearts,
    the peace into which you were also called in one Body.
And be thankful.
Let the word of Christ dwell in you richly,
    as in all wisdom you teach and admonish one another,
    singing psalms, hymns, and spiritual songs
    with gratitude in your hearts to God.
And whatever you do, in word or in deed,
    do everything in the name of the Lord Jesus,
    giving thanks to God the Father through him.

The word of the Lord.

D-9   (802-9)

Hebrews 13:1-4a, 5-6b   *Let marriage be held in honor by all.*

A reading from the Letter to the Hebrews

Brothers and sisters:
Let mutual love continue.
Do not neglect hospitality,
    for through it some have unknowingly entertained angels.

Be mindful of prisoners as if sharing their imprisonment,
and of the ill-treated as of yourselves,
for you are also in the body.
Let marriage be honored among all
and the marriage bed be kept undefiled.
Let your life be free from love of money
but be content with what you have,
for he has said, *I will never forsake you or abandon you.*
Thus we may say with confidence:

*The Lord is my helper,
and I will not be afraid.*

The word of the Lord.

D-10 (802-10)

1 Peter 3:1-9 *Be of one mind, sympathetic, loving toward one another.*

A reading from the first Letter of Saint Peter

Beloved:
You wives should be subordinate to your husbands so that,
even if some disobey the word,
they may be won over without a word by their wives' conduct
when they observe your reverent and chaste behavior.
Your adornment should not be an external one:
braiding the hair, wearing gold jewelry, or dressing in fine clothes,
but rather the hidden character of the heart,
expressed in the imperishable beauty
of a gentle and calm disposition,
which is precious in the sight of God.
For this is also how the holy women who hoped in God
once used to adorn themselves
and were subordinate to their husbands;
thus Sarah obeyed Abraham calling him "lord."
You are her children when do what is good
and fear no intimidation.

Likewise, you husbands should live with your wives in understanding,
    showing honor to the weaker female sex,
    since we are joint heirs of the gift of life,
    so that your prayers may not be hindered.

Finally, all of you, be of one mind, sympathetic,
    loving toward one another, compassionate, humble.
Do not return evil for evil, or insult for insult;
    but on the contrary, a blessing, because to this you were called,
    that you might inherit a blessing.

The word of the Lord.

D-11 (802-11)

1 John 3: 18-24   *Love in deed and in truth*

A reading from the first Letter of Saint John

Children, let us love not in word or speech
    but in deed and truth,
Now this is how we shall know that we belong to the truth
    and reassure our hearts before him
    in whatever our hearts condemn,
    for God is greater than our hearts and knows everything.
Beloved, if our hearts do not condemn us,
    we have confidence in God
    and receive from him whatever we ask,
    because we keep his commandments and do what pleases him.
And his commandment is this:
    we should believe in the name of his Son, Jesus Christ,
    and love one another just as he commanded us.
Those who keep his commandments remain in him, and he in them,
    and the way we know that he remains in us
    is from the Spirit that he gave us.

The word of the Lord.

D-12 (802-12)

1 John 4:7-12 *God is love.*

A reading from the first Letter of Saint John

Beloved, let us love one another,
    because love is of God;
    everyone who loves is begotten by God and knows God.
Whoever is without love does not know God, for God is love.
In this way the love of God was revealed to us:
    God sent his only-begotten Son into the world
    so that we might have life through him.
In this is love:
    not that we have loved God, but that he loved us
    and sent his Son as expiation for our sins.
Beloved, if God so loved us,
    we must also love one another.
No one has ever seen God.
Yet, if we love one another, God remains in us,
    and his love is brought to perfection in us.

The word of the Lord.

D-13 (802-13)

Revelation 19:1, 5-9a *Blessed are those who have been called to the wedding feast of the Lamb.*

A reading from the Book of Revelation

I, John, heard what sounded like the loud voice
    of a great multitude in heaven, saying:

    "Alleluia!
Salvation, glory, and might belong to our God."

A voice coming from the throne said:

"Praise our God, all you his servants,
and you who revere him, small and great."

Then I heard something like the sound of a great multitude
or the sound of rushing water or mighty peals of thunder,
as they said:
"Alleluia!
The Lord has established his reign,
our God, the almighty.
Let us rejoice and be glad
and give him glory.
For the wedding day of the Lamb has come,
his bride has made herself ready.
She was allowed to wear
a bright, clean linen garment."
(The linen represents the righteous deeds of the holy ones.)

Then the angel said to me,
"Write this:
Blessed are those who have been called
to the wedding feast of the Lamb."

The word of the Lord.

Alleluia Verse and Verse Before the Gospel

E-1 (804-1)

1 John 4:7b

Everyone who loves is begotten of God and knows God.

E-2 (804-2)

1 John 4:8b, 11

God is love.
If God loved us, we also must love one another.

E-3 (804-3)

1 John 4:12

If we love one another,
God remains in us,
and his love is brought to perfection in us.

E-4 (804-4)

1 John 4:16

Whoever remains in love,
remains in God and God in him.

Gospel

F-1 (805-1)

Matthew 5:1-12a   *Rejoice and be glad, for your reward will be great in heaven.*

A reading from the holy Gospel according to Matthew

When Jesus saw the crowds, he went up the mountain,
   and after he had sat down, his disciples came to him.
He began to teach them, saying:

   "Blessed are the poor in spirit,
      for theirs is the Kingdom of heaven.
   Blessed are they who mourn,
      for they will be comforted.
   Blessed are the meek,
      for they will inherit the land.
   Blessed are they who hunger and thirst for righteousness,
      for they will be satisfied.
   Blessed are the merciful,
      for they will be shown mercy.
   Blessed are the clean of heart,
      for they will see God.
   Blessed are the peacemakers,
      for they will be called children of God.
   Blessed are they who are persecuted for the sake of righteousness,
      for theirs is the Kingdom of heaven.
   Blessed are you when they insult you and persecute you
      and utter every kind of evil against you falsely because of me.
   Rejoice and be glad,
      for your reward will be great in heaven."

The Gospel of the Lord.

F-2 (805-2)

Matthew 5:13-16   *You are the light of the world.*

A reading from the holy Gospel according to Matthew

Jesus said to his disciples:
"You are the salt of the earth.
But if salt loses its taste, with what can it be seasoned?
It is no longer good for anything
   but to be thrown out and trampled underfoot.
You are the light of the world.
A city set on a mountain cannot be hidden.
Nor do they light a lamp and then put it under a bushel basket;
   it is set on a lamp stand,
   where it gives light to all in the house.
Just so, your light must shine before others,
   that they may see your good deeds
   and glorify your heavenly Father."

The Gospel of the Lord.

F-3 (805-3)

Long Form

Matthew 7:21, 24-29   *A wise man built his house on rock.*

A reading form the holy Gospel according to Matthew

Jesus said to his disciples:
"Not everyone who says to me, 'Lord, Lord,'
   will enter the Kingdom of heaven,
   but only the one who does the will of my Father in heaven.

"Everyone who listens to these words of mine and acts on them
   will be like a wise man who built his house on rock.
The rain fell, the floods came,
   and the winds blew and buffeted the house.

But it did not collapse; it had been set soldily on rock.
And everyone who listens to these words of mine
    but but does not act on them
    will be like a fool who built his house on sand.
The rain fell, the floods came,
    and the winds blew and buffeted the house.
And it collapsed and was completely ruined."
When Jesus finished these words,
    the crowds were astonished at his teaching,
    for he taught them as one having authority,
    and not as their scribes.

The Gospel of the Lord.

Or Short form

Matthew 7:21, 24-25   *A wise man built his house on rock.*

A reading from the holy Gospel according to Matthew

Jesus said to his disciples:
"Not everyone who says to me, 'Lord, Lord,'
    will enter the Kingdom of heaven,
    but only the one who does the will of my Father in heaven.

"Everyone who listens to these words of mine and acts on them
    will be like a wise man who built his house on rock.
The rain fell, the floods came,
    and the winds blew and buffeted the house.
But it did not collapse;
    it had been set solidly on rock."

The Gospel of the Lord.

F-4 (805-4)

Matthew 19:3-6 *What God has united, man must not separate.*

A reading from the holy Gospel according to Matthew

Some Pharisees approached Jesus, and tested him, saying
  "Is it lawful for a man to divorce his wife for any cause whatever?"
He said in reply, "Have you not read that from the beginning
  the Creator *made them male and female* and said ,
  For this reason a man shall leave his father and mother
  and be joined to his wife, and the two shall become one flesh?
So they are no longer two, but one flesh.
Therefore, what god has joined together, man must not separate."

The Gospel of the Lord.

F-5 (805-5)

Matthew 22:35-40 *This is the greatest and the first commandment. The second is like it.*

A reading from the holy Gospel according to Matthew

One of the Pharisees, a shcolar of the law, tested Jesus by asking,
  "Teacher, which commandment in the law is the greatest?"
He said to him,
  "You shall love the Lord, your God,
  with all your heart,
  with all your soul,
  and with all your mind.
This is the greatest and the first commandment.
The second is like it:
  You shall love your neighbor as yourself.
The whole law and the prophets depend on these two commandments."

The Gospel of the Lord.

F-6 (805-6)

Mark 10:6-9 *They are no longer two, but one flesh.*

A reading from the holy Gospel according to Mark

Jesus said:
"From the beginning of creation
   God made them male and female.
For this reason a man shall leave his father and mother
   and be joined to his wife,
   and the two shall become one flesh.
So they are no longer two but one flesh.
Therefore what God has joined together,
   no human being must separate.

The Gospel of the Lord.

F-7 (805-7)

John 2:1-11 *Jesus did this as the beginning of his signs in Cana in Galilee.*

A reading from the holy Gospel according to John

There was a wedding in Cana in Galilee,
   and the mother of Jesus was there.
Jesus and his disciples were also invited to the wedding.
When the wine ran short,
   the mother of Jesus said to him,
   "They have no wine."
And Jesus said to her,
   "Woman, how does your concern affect me?
My hour has not yet come."
His mother said to the servers,
   "Do whatever he tells you."
Now there were six stone water jars there for Jewish ceremonial washings,
   each holding twenty to thirty gallons.

Jesus told them,
   "Fill the jars with water."
So they filled them to the brim .
Then he told them,
   "Draw some out now and take it to the headwaiter."
So they took it.
And when the headwaiter tasted the water that had become wine,
   without knowing where it had come from
   (although the servants who had drawn the water knew),
   the headwaiter called the bridegroom and said to him,
   "Everyone serves good wine first,
   and then when people have drunk freely, an inferior one;
   but you have kept the good wine until now.
Jesus did this as the beginning of his signs in Cana in Galilee
   and so revealed his glory,
   and his disciples began to believe in him.

The Gospel of the Lord.

F-8 (805-8)

John 15: 9-12   *Remain in my love.*

A reading from the holy Gospel according to John

Jesus said to his disciples:
"As the Father loves me, so I also love you.
Remain in my love.
If you keep my commandments, you will remain in my love,
   just as I have kept my Father's commandments
   and remain in his love.
"I have told you this so that my joy might be in you
   and your joy might be complete.
This is my commandment: love one another as I love you."

The Gospel of the Lord.

F-9   (805-9)

John 15: 12-16   *This is my commandment: love one another.*

A reading from the holy Gospel according to John

Jesus said to his disciples;
"This is my commandment: love one another as I love you.
No one has greater love than this,
   to lay down one's life for one's friends.
You are my friends if you do what I command you.
I no longer call you slaves,
   because a slave does not know what his master is doing.
I have called you friends,
   because I have told you everything I have heard from my Father.
It was not you who chose me, but I who chose you
   and appointed you to go and bear fruit that will remain,
   so that whever you ask the Father in my name he may give you."

The Gospel of the Lord.

F-10   (805-10)

Long form

John 17:20-26   *That they may be brought to perfection as one.*

A reading from the holy Gospel according to John

Jesus raised his eyes to heaven and said:
"I pray not only for my disciples,
   but also for those who will believe in me through their word,
   so that they may all be one,
   as you, Father, are in me and I in you,
   that they also may be in us,
   that the world may believe that you sent me.
And I have given them the glory you gave me,

so that they may be one, as we are one,
I in them and you in me,
that they may be brought to perfection as one,
that the world may know that you sent me,
and that you loved them even as you loved me.
Father, they are your gift to me.
I wish that where I am they also may be with me,
that they may see my glory that you gave me,
because you loved me before the foundation of the world.
Righteous Father, the world also does not know you,
but I know you, and they know that you sent me.
I made known to them your name and I will make it known,
that the love with which you loved me
may be in them and I in them."

The Gospel of the Lord.

Or Short Form

John 17: 20-23   *That they may be brought to perfection as one.*

A reading form the holy Gospel according to John

Jesus raised his eyes to heaven and said:
"Holy Father, I pray not only for these,
but also for those who believe in me through their word,
so that they may all be one,
as you, Father, are in me and I in you,
that they also may be in us,
that the world may believe that you sent me.
And I have given them the glory you gave me,
so that they may be one, as we are one,
I in them and you in me,
that they may be brought to perfection as one,
that the world may know that you sent me,
and that you loved them even as you loved me."

The Gospel of the Lord.

Homily

RITE OF MARRIAGE (During Mass)

All stand, including the bride and bridegroom, and the priest addresses them in these or similar words:

My dear friends, you have come together in this church so that the Lord may seal and strengthen your love in the presence of the Church's minister and this community. Christ abundantly blesses this love. He has already consecrated you in baptism and now he enriches and strengthens you by a special sacrament so that you may assume the duties of marriage in mutual and lasting fidelity. And so, in the presence of the Church, I ask you to state your intentions.

Intentions

The priest then questions them about their freedom of choice, faithfulness to each other, and the acceptance and upbringing of children:

N. and N. have you come here freely and without reservation to give yourselves to each other in marriage?

Will you love and honor each other as man and wife for the rest of your lives?

The following question may be omitted if, for example, the couple is advanced in years.

Will you accept children lovingly from God, and bring them up according to the law of Christ and his Church?

Each answers the questions separately.

Consent

The priest invites the couple to declare their consent:

Since it is your intention to enter into marriage, join your right hands, and declare your consent before God and his Church.

They join hands.

The bridegroom says:

I, N., take you, N., to be my wife. I promise to be true to you in good times and in bad, in sickness and in health. I will love you and honor you all the days of my life.

The bride says:

I, *N.*, take you, *N.*, to be my husband. I promise to be true to you in good times and in bad, in sickness and in health. I will love you and honor you all the days of my life.

H-2

In dioceses of the United States the following form may be used:
The bridegroom says:

I, *N.*, take you *N.*, for my lawful wife, to have to to hold, from this day forward, for better, for worse, for richer, for poorer, in sickness and in health, until death do us part.

The bride says:

I, *N.*, take you, *N.*, for my lawful husband, to have and to hold, from this day forward, for better, for worse, for richer, for poorer, in sickness and in health, until death do us part.

If, however, it seems preferable for pastoral reasons, the priest may obtain consent from the couple through questions.

First he asks the bridegroom:

N., do you take N. to be your wife? Do you promise to be true to her in good times and in bad, in sickness and in health, to love her and honor her all the days of your life?

The bridegroom: **I do.**

Then he asks the bride:

N., do you take N. to be your husband? Do you promise to be true to him in good times and in bad, in sickness and in health, to love him and honor him all the days of your life?

The bride: **I do.**

In dioceses of the United States the following form may be used:

First he asks the bridegroom:

N., do you take N. for your lawful wife, to have and to hold, from this day forward, for better, for worse, for richer, for poorer, in sickness and in health, until death do you part?

The bridegroom: I do.

Then he asks the bride:

N., do you take N. for your lawful husband, to have and to hold, from this day forward, for better, for worse, for richer, for poorer, in sickness and in health, until death do you part?

The bride: I do.

Receiving their consent, the priest says:
You have declared your consent before the Church.
May the Lord in his goodness strengthen your consent
and fill you both with his blessings.
What God has joined, men must not divide.
R. Amen.

Blessing and Exchange of Rings

Priest:

I-1

May the Lord bless + these rings
which you give to each other
as the sign of your love and fidelity.
R. Amen.

I-2

Lord, bless these rings which we bless + in your name.
Grant that those who wear them
may always have a deep faith in each other.

May they do your will
and always live together
in peace, good will, and love.

We ask this through Christ our Lord.
R. Amen.

I-3

Lord,
bless + and consecrate *N.* and *N.*
in their love for each other.
May these rings be a symbol
of true faith in each other,
and always remind them of their love.

We ask this through Christ our Lord.
R. Amen.

The bridegroom places his wife's ring on her ring finger. He may say:

N., take this ring as a sign of my love and fidelity. In the name of the Father, and of the Son, and of the Holy Spirit.

The bride places her husband's ring on his finger. She may say:

N., take this ring as a sign of my love and fidelity. In the name of the Father, and of the Son, and of the Holy Spirit.

Prayer of the Faithful

The general intercessions (prayer of the faithful) follow, using formulas approved by the conference of bishops. Since the Rite of Marriage does not provide any official General Intercessions, these are provided as a sample. Consult your priest about using other intercessions or writing your own.

Priest:

Now that we have heard God's word in the Bible and felt his presence in this exchange of vows, let us present to God the Father these petitions for people in the world today.

Reader: The response is "Lord, hear our prayer." For our Holy Father on earth, the Pope, all the bishops and the clergy everywhere, that they may lead us to a deeper faith in God and a stronger love for others, let us pray to the Lord.

R. Lord, hear our prayer.

Reader: For our president and all leaders of government, that what they do may not harm true family life, let us pray to the Lord.

R. Lord, hear our prayer.

Reader: For all married persons, that they will be faithful to God and to each other, let us pray to the Lord.

R. Lord, hear our prayer.

Reader: For N. and N., that they will always give God first place in their lives, that they will enjoy the support of friends and the blessing of children, let us pray to the Lord.

R. Lord, hear our prayer.

Reader: That N. and N. and their children will be a source of inspiration and support to those around them, let us pray to the Lord.

R. Lord, hear our prayer.

Reader: For N. and N.'s ancestors, both living and dead, and for all who helped them to grow in faith, let us pray to the Lord.

R. Lord, hear our prayer.

Reader: For a rebirth of chastity and a stop to abortion, let us pray to the Lord.

R. Lord, hear our prayer.

Reader: For the heartfelt petitions of each one here (pause), let us pray to the Lord.

R. Lord, hear our prayer.

Priest: O God our Father in heaven, your Son taught us to ask, to seek and to knock. We have just done so, confident that you will now look upon our many needs, consider our trusting faith, and in your great love grant these requests which we present to you through Jesus Christ our Lord.

R. Amen.

LITURGY OF THE EUCHARIST

Prayer Over the Gifts

With hands extended, the priest sings or says one of the following:

K-1

**Lord,
accept our offering
for this newly-married couple, *N.* and *N.*
By your love and providence you have brought them together;
now bless them all the days of their married life.**

We ask this through Christ our Lord.
R. **Amen.**

K-2

**Lord,
accept the gifts we offer you
on this happy day.
In your fatherly love watch over and protect *N.* and *N.*,
whom you have united in marriage.**

We ask this though Christ our Lord.
R. **Amen.**

K-3

**Lord,
hear our prayers
and accept the gifts we offer for *N.* and *N.*
Today you have made them one in the sacrament of marriage.
May the mystery of Christ's unselfish love,
which we celebrate in this eucharist,
increase their love for you and for each other.**

We ask this through Christ our Lord.
R. **Amen.**

Preface

The priest begins the eucharistic prayer. With hands extended, he sings or says:

L-1

The Lord be with you.
R. And also with you.

Life up your hearts.
R. We lift them up to the Lord.

Let us give thanks to the Lord our God.
R. It is right to give him thanks and praise.

Father, all-powerful and ever-living God,
we do well always and everywhere to give you thanks.
By this sacrament your grace unites man and woman
in an unbreakable bond of love and peace.

You have designed the chaste love of husband and wife
for the increase both of the human family
and of your own family born in baptism.

You are the loving Father of the world of nature;
you are the loving Father of the new creation of grace.
In Christian marriage you bring together
    the two orders of creation:
nature's gift of children enriches the world
and your grace enriches also your Church.

Through Christ the choirs of angels
    and all the saints
    praise and worship your glory.
May our voices blend with theirs
as we join in the unending hymn:

Holy, holy, holy Lord, God of power and might,
heaven and earth are full of your glory.
    Hosanna in the highest.
Blessed is he who comes in the name of the Lord.
    Hosanna in the highest.

L-2

The Lord be with you.
R. And also with you.

Lift up your hearts.
R. We lift them up to the Lord.

Let us give thanks to the Lord our God.
R. It is right to give him thanks and praise.

Father, all-powerful and ever-living God,
we do well always and everywhere to give you thanks
through Jesus Christ our Lord.

Through him you entered into a new covenant with your people.
You restored man to grace in the saving mystery of redemption.
You gave him a share in the divine life
through his union with Christ.
You made him an heir of Christ's eternal glory.

This outpouring of love in the new covenant of grace
is symbolized in the marriage covenant
that seals the love of husband and wife
and reflects your divine plan of love.

And so, with the angels and all the saints in heaven
we proclaim your glory
and join in their unending hymn of praise:

Holy, holy, holy Lord, God of power and might,
heaven and earth are full of your glory.
   Hosanna in the highest.
Blessed is he who comes in the name of the Lord.
   Hosanna in the highest.

L-3

The Lord be with you.
R. And also with you.

Lift up your hearts.
R. We lift them up to the Lord.

Let us give thanks to the Lord our God.
R. It is right to give him thanks and praise.

Father, all-powerful and ever-living God,
we do well always and everywhere to give you thanks.

You created man in love to share your divine life.
We see his high destiny in the love of husband and wife,
which bears the imprint of your own divine love.

Love is man's origin,
love is his constant calling,
love is his fulfillment in heaven.

The love of man and woman
is made holy in the sacrament of marriage,
and becomes the mirror of your everlasting love.

Through Christ the choirs of angels
and all the saints
praise and worship your glory.
May our voices blend with theirs
as we join in their unending hymn:

Holy, holy, holy Lord, God of power and might,
heaven and earth are full of your glory.
    Hosanna in the highest.
Blessed is he who comes in the name of the Lord.
    Hosanna in the highest.

EUCHARISTIC PRAYER I, II, III, or IV

COMMUNION RITE

The Lord's Prayer
Nuptial Blessing

After the Lord's Prayer, the prayer Deliver us *is omitted. The priest faces the bride and bridegroom and, with hands joined, says:*

M-1

My dear friends, let us turn to the Lord and pray
that he will bless with his grace this woman *(or N.)*
now married in Christ to this man *(or N.)*
and that (through the sacrament of the body and blood of Christ,)
he will unite in love the couple he has joined in this holy bond.

*All pray silently for a short while. Then the priest extends his hands and
continues:*

Father, by your power you have made everything out of nothing.
In the beginning you created the universe
and made mankind in your own likeness.
You gave man the constant help of woman
so that man and woman should no longer be two, but one flesh,
and you teach us that what you have united
may never be divided.

Father, you have made the union of man and wife so holy a mystery
that it symbolizes the marriage of Christ and his Church.

Father, by your plan man and woman are united,
and married life has been established
as the one blessing that was not forfeited by original sin
or washed away in the flood.

Look with love upon this woman, your daughter,
now joined to her husband in marriage.
She asks your blessing.
Give her the grace of love and peace.
May she always follow the example of the holy women
whose praises are sung in the scriptures.

May her husband put his trust in her
and recognize that she is his equal
and the heir with him to the life of grace.
May he always honor her and love her
as Christ loves his bride, the Church.

162

Father, keep them always true to your commandments.
Keep them faithful in marriage
and let them be living examples of Christian life.

Give them the strength which comes from the gospel
so that they may be witnesses of Christ to others.
(Bless them with children and help them to be good parents.
May they live to see their children's children.)
And, after a happy old age,
grant them fullness of life with the saints
in the kingdom of heaven.

We ask this through Christ our Lord.

R. Amen.

If one or both of the parties will not be receiving communion, the words in the introduction to the nuptial blessing, through the sacrament of the body and blood of Christ, *may be omitted.*

If desired, in the prayer Father, by your power, *two of the first three paragraphs may be omitted, keeping only the paragraph which corresponds to the reading of the Mass.*

In the last paragraph of this prayer, the words in parentheses may be omitted whenever circumstances suggest it, if, for example, the couple is advanced in years.

Other forms of the nuptial blessing:

M-2

In the following prayer, either the paragraph Holy Father, you created mankind *or the paragraph* Father, to reveal the plan of your love, *may be omitted, keeping only the paragraph which corresponds to the reading of the Mass.*

Let us pray to the Lord for *N.* **and** *N.*
who come to God's altar at the beginning of their married life
so that they may always be united in love for each other
(as now they share in the body and blood of Christ).

All pray silently for a short while. Then the priest extends his hands and continues:

Holy Father, you created mankind in your own image
and made man and woman to be joined as husband and wife
in union of body and heart
and so fulfill their mission in this world.

Father, to reveal the plan of your love,
you made the union of husband and wife
an image of the covenant between you and your people.
In the fulfillment of this sacrament,
the marriage of Christian man and woman
is a sign of the marriage between Christ and the Church.
Father, stretch out your hand, and bless *N.* and *N.*

Lord, grant that as they begin to live this sacrament
they may share with each other the gifts of your love
and become one in heart and mind
as witnesses to your presence in their marriage.
Help them to create a home together
(and give them children to be formed by the gospel
and to have a place in your family).

Give your blessing to *N.*, your daughter,
so that she may be a good wife (and mother),
caring for the home,
faithful in love for her husband,
generous and kind.
Give your blessings to *N.*, your son,
so that he may be a faithful husband
(and a good father).

Father, grant that as they come together to your table on earth,
so they may one day have the joy of sharing your feast in heaven.

We ask this through Christ our Lord.

R. Amen.

M-3

My dear friends, let us ask God
for his continued blessings upon this bridegroom and his bride *(or N. and N.)*.

All pray silently for a short while. Then the priest extends his hands and continues:

Holy Father, creator of the universe,
maker of man and woman in your own likeness,
source of blessing for married life,
we humbly pray to you for this woman
who today is united with her husband in this sacrament of marriage.

May your fullest blessing come upon her and her husband
so that they may together rejoice in your gift of married love
(and enrich your Church with their children).

Lord, may they both praise you when they are happy
and turn to you in their sorrows.
May they be glad that you help them in their work
and know that you are with them in their need.
May they pray to you in the community of the Church,
and be your witnesses in the world.
May they reach old age in the company of their friends,
and come at last to the kingdom of heaven.

We ask this through Christ our Lord.

R. Amen.

The Sign of Peace
Communion
Prayer After Communion

Lord,
in your love you have given us this eucharist
to unite us with one another and with you.
As you have made *N.* and *N.*
one in this sacrament of marriage
(and in the sharing of the one bread and the one cup),
so now make them one in love for each other.

We ask this through Christ our Lord.

R. Amen.

N-2

Lord, we who have shared the food of your table
pray for our friends N. and N.
whom you have joined together in marriage.
Keep them close to you always.
May their love for each other
proclaim to all the world
their faith in you.

We ask this through Christ our Lord.

R. Amen.

N-3

Almighty God,
may the sacrifice we have offered
and the eucharist we have shared
strengthen the love of N. and N.,
and give us all your fatherly aid.

We ask this through Christ our Lord.

R. Amen.

CONCLUDING RITE

Solemn or Final Blessing

*Before blessing the people at the end of Mass, the priest blesses the bride
and bridegroom, using one of the forms below:*

O-1

God the eternal Father keep you in love with each other,
so that the peace of Christ may stay with you
and be always in your home.

R. Amen.

May (your children bless you,)
your friends console you
and all men live in peace with you.

R. Amen.

May you always bear witness to the love of God in this world
so that the afflicted and the needy
will find in you generous friends,
and welcome you into the joys of heaven.

R. Amen.

And may almighty God bless you all,
the Father, and the Son, + and the Holy Spirit.

R. Amen.

May God, the almighty Father,
give you his joy
and bless you (in your children).

R. Amen.

May the only Son of God have mercy on you
and help you in good times and in bad.

R. Amen.

May the Holy Spirit of God
always fill your hearts with his love.

R. Amen.

And may almighty God bless you all,
the Father, and the Son, + and the Holy Spirit.

R. Amen.

O-3

May the Lord Jesus, who was a guest at the wedding in Cana,
bless you and your families and friends.

R. Amen.

May Jesus, who loved his Church to the end,
always fill your hearts with his love.

R. Amen.

May he grant that, as you believe in his resurrection,
so you may wait for him in joy and hope.

R. Amen.

And may almighty God bless you all,
the Father, and the Son, + and the Holy Spirit.

R. Amen.

O-4

In the diocese of the United States the following form may be used:

May Almighty God, with his Word of blessing,
unite your hearts in the never-ending bond of pure love.

R. Amen.

May your children bring you happiness,
and may your generous love for them be returned to you,
many times over.

R. Amen.

May the peace of Christ live always in your hearts
and in your home.
May you have true friends to stand by you,
both in joy and in sorrow.
May you be ready and willing to help and comfort
all who come to you in need.
And may the blessings promised to the compassionate
be yours in abundance.

R. Amen.

May you find happiness and satisfaction in your work.
May daily problems never cause you undue anxiety,
nor the desire for earthly possessions dominate your lives.
But may your hearts' first desire be always
the good things waiting for you in the life of heaven.

R. Amen.

May the Lord bless you with many happy years together,
so that you may enjoy the rewards of a good life.
And after you have served him loyally in his kingdom on earth,
may he welcome you to his eternal kingdom in heaven.

R. Amen.

And may almighty God bless you all,
the Father, and the Son, + and the Holy Spirit.

R. Amen.

Dismissal

Rite for Celebrating Marriage Outside Mass

Introductory Rites
Liturgy of the Word
See Readings on pages 117-152 in "Rite for Celebrating Marriage During Mass."

RITE OF MARRIAGE
All stand, including the bride and bridegroom, and the priest addresses them in these or similar words:

My dear friends, you have come together in this church so that the Lord may seal and strengthen your love in the presence of the Church's minister and this community. Christ abundantly blesses this love. He has already consecrated you in baptism and now he enriches and strengthens you by a special sacrament so that you may assume the duties of marriage in mutual and lasting fidelity. And so, in the presence of the Church, I ask you to state your intentions.

Intentions
The priest then questions them about their freedom of choice, faithfulness to each other, and the acceptance and upbringing of children:

N. and N., have you come here freely and without reservation to give yourselves to each other in marriage?

Will you love and honor each other as man and wife for the rest of your lives?

The following question may be omitted if, for example, the couple is advanced in years.

Will you accept children lovingly from God, and bring them up according to the law of Christ and his Church?

Each answers the questions separately.

Consent

The priest invites them to declare their consent:

Since it is your intention to enter into marriage, join your right hands, and declare your consent before God and his Church.

They join hands.

H-1

The bridegroom says:

I, *N.*, take you, *N.*, to be my wife. I promise to be true to you in good times and in bad, in sickness and in health. I will love you and honor you all the days of my life.

The bride says:

I, *N.*, take you, *N.*, to be my husband. I promise to be true to you in good times and in bad, in sickness and in health. I will love you and honor you all the days of my life.

H-2

In dioceses of the United States the following form may be used:

The bridegroom says:

I, *N.*, take you, *N.*, for my wife, to have and to hold, from this day forward, for better, for worse, for richer, for poorer, in sickness and in health, until death do us part.

The bride says:

I, *N.*, take you, *N.*, for my husband, to have and to hold, from this day forward, for better, for worse, for richer, for poorer, in sickness and in health, until death do us part.

If, however, it seems preferable for pastoral reasons, the priest may obtain consent from the couple through questions.

First he asks the bridegroom:

N., do you take *N.* to be your wife? Do you promise to be true to her in good times and in bad, in sickness and in health, to love her and honor her all the days of your life?

The bridegroom: **I do.**
Then he asks the bride:

N., do you take *N.* to be your husband? Do you promise to be true to him in good times and in bad, in sickness and in health, to love him and honor him all the days of your life?

The bride: **I do.**

In dioceses of the United States the following form may be used:
First he asks the bridegroom:

N., do you take *N.* for your lawful wife, to have and to hold, from this day forward, for better, for worse, for richer, for poorer, in sickness and health, until death do you part?

The bridegroom: **I do.**

Then he asks the bride:

N., do you take *N.* for your lawful husband, to have and to hold, from this day forward, for better, for worse, for richer, for poorer, in sickness and health, until death do you part?

The bride: **I do.**

Receiving their consent, the priest says:

You have declared your consent before the Church. May the Lord in his goodness strengthen your consent and fill you both with his blessings. What God has joined, men must not divide.

R. **Amen.**

Blessing and Exchange of Rings

Priest:

May the Lord bless + these rings which you give to each other as the sign of your love and fidelity.

R. **Amen.**

Note: For other forms of this blessing, see pages 155-156.

The bridegroom places his wife's ring on her ring finger.
He may say:

***N.*, take this ring as a sign of my love and fidelity.**
In the name of the Father, and of the Son, and of the Holy Spirit.

The bride places her husband's ring on his ring finger.
She may say:

***N.*, take this ring as a sign of my love and fidelity.**
In the name of the Father, and of the Son, and of the Holy Spirit.

General Intercessions

The general intercessions (prayer of the faithful) and the blessing of the couple take place in this order: a) invitatory of any blessing [see first part of M1, page 161; M2, page 163; M3, page 164]; b) petitions; c) nuptial blessing without the invitatory.

If the rubrics call for it, the profession of faith is said after the general intercessions.

Nuptial Blessings

See Nuptial Blessings on pages 161-165 in "Rite for Celebrating Marriage During Mass."

Conclusion of the Celebration

The Lord's Prayer
Blessing

See Concluding Rites on page 166-169 in "Rite for Celebrating Marriage During Mass."

Rite of Marriage
(Catholic and Unbaptized Person)

Introductory Rites

Liturgy of the Word

See Readings on pages 117-152 in "Rite for Celebrating Marriage During Mass."

MARRIAGE RITE

All stand, including the bride and the bridegroom. The priest addresses them in these or similar words:

My dear friends, you have come together in this church so that the Lord may seal and strengthen your love in the presence of the Church's minister and this community. In this way you will be strengthened to keep mutual and lasting faith with each other and to carry out the other duties of marriage. And so, in the presence of the Church, I ask you to state your intentions.

Intentions

The priest then questions them about their freedom of choice, faithfulness to each other, and the acceptance and upbringing of children:

N. and N., have you come here freely and without reservation to give yourselves to each other in marriage? Will you love and honor each other as man and wife for the rest of your lives?

The following question may be omitted if, for example, the couple is advanced in years:

Will you accept children lovingly from God, and bring them up according to the law of Christ and his Church?

Each answers the questions separately.

Consent

The priest invites them to declare their consent:

Since it is your intention to enter into marriage, join your right hands, and declare your consent before God and his Church.

They join hands.

H-1

The bridegroom says:

I, *N.*, take you, *N.*, to be my wife. I promise to be true to you in good times and in bad, in sickness and in health: I will love you and honor you all the days of my life.

The bride says:

I, *N.*, take you, *N.*, to be my husband. I promise to be true to you in good times and in bad, in sickness and in health: I will love you and honor you all the days of my life.

H-2

In dioceses of the United States the following form may be used:

The bridegroom says:

I, *N.*, take you, *N.*, for my lawful wife, to have and to hold, from this day forward, for better, for worse, for richer, for poorer, in sickness and in health, until death do us part.

The bride says:

I, *N.*, take you, *N.*, for my lawful husband, to have and to hold, from this day forward, for better, for worse, for richer, for poorer, in sickness and in health, until death do us part.

If, however, it seems preferable for pastoral reasons, the priest may obtain consent from the couple through questions.

First he asks the bridegroom:

N., do you take N. to be your wife? Do you promise to be true to her in good times and in bad, in sickness and in health, to love her and honor her all the days of your life?

The bridegroom: **I do.**

Then he asks the bride:

N., do you take N. to be your husband? Do you promise to be true to him in good times and in bad, in sickness and in health, to love him and honor him all the days of your life?

The bride: **I do.**

In dioceses of the United States the following form may be used:

First he asks the bridegroom:

N., do you take N. for your lawful wife, to have and to hold, from this day forward, for better, for worse, for richer, for poorer, in sickness and in health, until death do you part?

The bridegroom: **I do.**

Then he asks the bride:

N., do you take N. for your lawful husband, to have and to hold, from this day forward, for better, for worse, for richer, for poorer, in sickness and in health, until death do you part?

The bride: **I do.**

Receiving their consent, the priest says:

You have declared your consent before the Church. May the Lord in his goodness strengthen your consent and fill you both with his blessings. What God has joined, men must not divide.

R. **Amen.**

Blessing and Exchange of Rings

If circumstances so require, the blessing and exchange of rings can be omitted. If this rite is observed, the priest says:

**May the Lord bless + these rings
which you give to each other
as the sign of your love and fidelity.**

R. **Amen.**

Note: For other forms of the blessing of rings, see pages 155-156.

The bridegroom places his wife's ring on her ring finger. He may say:

N., take this ring as a sign of my love and fidelity. In the name of the Father, and of the Son, and of the Holy Spirit.

The bride places her husband's ring on his ring finger. She may say:

N., take this ring as a sign of my love and fidelity. In the name of the Father, and of the Son, and of the Holy Spirit.

General Intercessions

The general intercessions (prayer of the faithful) and the blessing of the couple take place in this order: a) invitatory of any blessing [see first part of M1, page 161; M2, page 163; M3, page 164]; b) petitions; c) nuptial blessing without the invitatory.

If the rubrics call for it, the profession of faith is said after the general intercessions.

Nuptial Blessing

Facing them, the priest joins his hands and says:

My brothers and sisters, let us ask God for his continued blessings upon this bridegroom and his bride.

All pray silently for a short while. Then the priest extends his hands and continues:

Holy Father, creator of the universe,
maker of man and woman in your own likeness,
source of blessing for the married life,
we humbly pray to you for this bride
who today is united with her husband
in the bond of marriage.

May your fullest blessing come upon her and her husband
so that they may together rejoice in your gift of married love.
May they be noted for their good lives,
(and be parents filled with virtue).

Lord, may they both praise you when they are happy
and turn to you in their sorrows.
May they be glad that you help them in their work,
and know that you are with them in their need.

**May they reach old age in the company of their friends,
and come at last to the kingdom of heaven.**

We ask this through Christ our Lord.

R. **Amen.**

Conclusion of the Celebration

The Lord's Prayer
Blessing
See Concluding Rite, pages 166-169.

Selection Record
Marriage Within Mass

*To the Couple: After you have selected the readings, prayers and blessings for your Wedding Mass, indicate them on this form in the proper places. Then **photocopy this form (this page and next) and give the copy to the priest or deacon** for his information in preparing for the wedding ceremony. If you make selections other than those listed, include that information in the final section on this form.*

Entrance Procession: (check or fill in)

_____ Procession with ministers

_____ Ushers, Bridesmaids, Maid or Matron of Honor, Bride and Father

_____ Both parents accompany the Bride

_____ Both Bride and Groom accompanied by parents down main aisle preceded by Ushers and Bridesmaids

_____ Other:_____

_____

Opening Prayer: pages 115-116

_____, page _____

Old Testament Reading: pages 117-125

_____, page _____

Read by_____

Responsorial Psalm: pages 125-131

_____, page _____

Read/sung by_____

New Testament Reading: pages 131-143

_____, page _____

Read by_____

Alleluia Verse: page 144

_____,   Sung _____   Omitted _____

Sung by_____

Gospel: pages 145-152

_____, page _____

Read by_____

Exchange of Consent or Wedding Vows: pages 153-155

_____, page _____

Consent through questions _____   Memorized _____

Recited after priest _____   Read from book _____

Blessing of Rings: page 155-156

_____, page _____

Double-ring ceremony _____   Single-ring ceremony _____

Prayer of the Faithful:

read by_____

Presentation of the Gifts:

Brought forward by: Bride and Groom _____   Parents _____

     Best Man and Maid of Honor _____   Others _____

Symbolic Gift for the Poor: Yes _____   No _____

Prayer Over the Gifts: page 158

_____, page _____

Preface: pages 159-161

_____, page _____

Nuptial Blessing: pages 161-165

_____, page _____

Sign of Peace:

Bride and Groom only _____   Couple to wedding party _____

Couple to wedding party and parents _____

Couple to wedding party, parents and guests down main aisle _____

Communion:

Groom _____   Bride _____   Best Man _____

Maid or Matron of Honor _____

Under both kinds: Yes _____   No _____

Prayer After Communion: pages 165-166

_____, page _____

Final Blessing: pages 166-169

_____, page _____

Other Special Elements or Alternatives:

_____

_____

_____

_____

Selection Record
Marriage Outside Mass

To the Couple: After you have selected the readings, prayers and blessings for your Wedding Ceremony, indicate them on this form in the proper places. **Then photocopy this form (this page and next) and give the copy to the priest or deacon** *for his information in preparing for the wedding ceremony. If you make selections other than those listed, include that information in the final section on this form.*

Entrance Procession: (check or fill in)

_____ Procession with ministers

_____ Ushers, Bridesmaids, Maid or Matron of Honor, Bride and Father

_____ Both parents accompany the Bride

_____ Both Bride and Groom accompanied by parents down main aisle preceded by Ushers and Bridesmaids

_____ Other:_____

_____

Opening Prayer: (optional) pages 115-116

_____, page _____

Old Testament Reading: pages 117-125

_____, page _____

Read by_____

Responsorial Psalm: pages 125-131

_____, page _____

Read/sung by_____

New Testament Reading: pages 131-143

_____, page _____

Read by_____

Alleluia Verse: page 144

_____,   Sung _____   Omitted _____

Sung by_____

Gospel: pages 145-152

_____, page _____

Read by_____

Exchange of Consent or Wedding Vows: pages 170-172

_____, page _____

Consent through questions _____   Memorized _____

Recited after priest _____   Read from book _____

Blessing of Rings: page 173

Double-ring ceremony _____   Single-ring ceremony _____

Prayer of the Faithful

read by_____

Nuptial Blessing: pages 161-165

_____, page _____

Final Blessing: pages 166-169

_____, page _____

Other Special Elements or Alternatives:

_____

_____

_____

_____

Selection Record
Marriage Between Catholic and Unbaptized Person

*To the Couple: After you have selected the prayers and blessings for your Wedding Ceremony, indicate them on this form in the proper places. Then **photocopy this form (this page and next) and give the copy to the priest or deacon** for his information in preparing for the wedding ceremony. If you make selections other than those listed, include that information in the final section on this form.*

Entrance Procession: (check or fill in)

_____ Procession with ministers

_____ Ushers, Bridesmaids, Maid or Matron of Honor, Bride and Father

_____ Both parents accompany the Bride

_____ Both Bride and Groom accompanied by parents down main aisle preceded by Ushers and Bridesmaids

_____ Other:_____

_____

Opening Prayer: (optional) pages 115-116

_____, page _____

Old Testament Reading: pages 117-125

_____, page _____

Read by_____

Responsorial Psalm: pages 125-131

_____, page _____

Read/sung by_____

New Testament Reading: pages 131-143

_____, page _____

Read by_____

Alleluia Verse: page 144

_____,   Sung _____   Omitted _____

Sung by_____

Gospel: pages 145-152

_____, page _____

Read by_____

Exchange of Consent or Wedding Vows: pages 174-176

_____, page _____

Consent through questions _____   Memorized _____

Recited after priest _____   Read from book _____

Final Blessing: pages 166-169

_____, page _____

Other Special Elements or Alternatives in Our Ceremony:

_____

_____

_____

_____

_____

_____

_____

_____

_____

_____

_____

_____

_____

Wedding Party
Information

Bridegroom: _____

Bride: _____

Priest or Deacon: _____

Church: _____

Date of Celebration_____   Time: _____

Best Man:_____

Maid or Matron of Honor:_____

Number of Ushers:_____   Number of Bridesmaids:_____

Ring Bearer: Yes_____   No _____

Flower Girl: Yes_____   No _____   How many: _____

Rehearsal Date: _____   Time: _____

Organist Contacted: Yes_____   No _____

Other Musicians: Yes_____ No _____

Altar Servers: Couple provides_____ Church provides_____